$3 ?? 12.95

Thomas Wolfe

LITERATURE AND LIFE SERIES

(Formerly *Modern Literature* and *World Dramatists*)

GENERAL EDITOR: Philip Winsor

Selected list of titles:

SHERWOOD ANDERSON   *Welford Dunaway Taylor*
JAMES BALDWIN   *Carolyn Wedin Sylvander*
SAUL BELLOW   *Brigitte Scheer-Schäzler*
ANTHONY BURGESS   *Samuel Coale*
TRUMAN CAPOTE   *Helen S. Garson*
WILLA CATHER   *Dorothy Tuck McFarland*
JOHN CHEEVER   *Samuel Coale*
JOSEPH CONRAD   *Martin Tucker*
JOAN DIDION   *Katherine Usher Henderson*
JOHN DOS PASSOS   *George J. Becker*
THEODORE DREISER   *James Lundquist*
T. S. ELIOT   *Burton Raffel*
WILLIAM FAULKNER   *Joachim Seyppel*
F. SCOTT FITZGERALD   *Rose Adrienne Gallo*
FORD MADOX FORD   *Sondra J. Stang*
E. M. FORSTER   *Claude J. Summers*
JOHN FOWLES   *Barry N. Olshen*
ROBERT FROST   *Elaine Barry*
ELLEN GLASGOW   *Marcelle Thiébaux*
ROBERT GRAVES   *Katherine Snipes*
ERNEST HEMINGWAY   *Samuel Shaw*
JOHN IRVING   *Gabriel Miller*
CHRISTOPHER ISHERWOOD   *Claude J. Summers*
SARAH ORNE JEWETT   *Josephine Donovan*
JAMES JOYCE   *Armin Arnold*
KEN KESEY   *Barry H. Leeds*
RING LARDNER   *Elizabeth Evans*
D. H. LAWRENCE   *George J. Becker*
C. S. LEWIS   *Margaret Patterson Hannay*
SINCLAIR LEWIS   *James Lundquist*
ROBERT LOWELL   *Burton Raffel*
NORMAN MAILER   *Philip H. Bufithis*
BERNARD MALAMUD   *Sheldon J. Hershinow*
MARY MCCARTHY   *Willene Schaefer Hardy*
CARSON MCCULLERS   *Richard M. Cook*
JAMES A. MICHENER   *George J. Becker*

(continued on last page of book)

Thomas Wolfe

Elizabeth Evans

FREDERICK UNGAR PUBLISHING CO.
New York

Copyright © 1984 by Frederick Ungar Publishing Co., Inc.
Printed in the United States of America
Design by Jeremiah B. Lighter

Library of Congress Cataloging in Publication Data

Evans, Elizabeth, 1935—
  Thomas Wolfe.

  (Literature and life series)
    1. Wolfe, Thomas, 1900–1938. 2. Novelists, American
—20th century—Biography. I. Title. II. Series.
PS3545.337Z68 1983   813'.52 [B]   82-40275
ISBN 0-8044-2188-9

Grateful acknowledgment is made to Thomas Noonan of the Harvard College Library, H. G. Jones of the University of North Carolina Library, and Andrea Brown of the St. Mary's College Library for their assistance in my use of their respective Thomas Wolfe collections.

I am indebted to Paul Gitlin, Executor of the Estate of Thomas Wolfe, for permission to work in these collections and to quote from them in this monograph.

I owe thanks to the Georgia Tech Foundation for research grants needed to complete this study.

Finally, I am most grateful to Dr. Sarah Gordon, Georgia College, Milledgeville, Georgia, for expert editorial advice.

Acknowledgment to Charles Scribner's Sons for permission to quote excerpts and passages from copyrighted works by Thomas Wolfe and others, including among those cited in the bibliography: *Look Homeward, Angel; Of Time and the River; The Letters of Thomas Wolfe; The Face of a Nation; A Stone, A Leaf, A Door;* and *From Death to Morning.* I am also grateful to Scribner's and to the University of North Carolina for permission to quote portions from the Max Perkins material found in the John Terry papers in the Thomas Wolfe Collection at the University of North Carolina at Chapel Hill.

After the first citation, subsequent quotations use a shortened form and are cited parenthetically in the text.

In memory of
C. Hugh Holman

Contents

Chronology   ix

1

The Writer from Asheville   1

2

Look Homeward, Angel
and *Of Time and the River:*
"The Apple Tree, the Singing,
and the Gold"   35

3

The Web and the Rock and
You Can't Go Home Again:
Novels of Magnificent Fragments   65

4

From Death to Morning,
The Hills Beyond, and
The Short Novels:
Failure, Success?   95

5

"My Name Is Wolfe: I Am
an American"   135

Notes   165

Bibliography   177

Index   187

Chronology

1900   On October 3, Thomas Clayton Wolfe
        is born in Asheville, North Carolina, to
        Julia Westall and W. O. Wolfe.

1904   Goes with mother and older siblings to
        St. Louis and the World's Fair; Mrs.
        Wolfe runs a summer boarding house;
        brother Grover Wolfe dies.

1905   Enters Asheville's Orange Street Public
        School.

1912   Begins classes at the private North
        State Fitting School, run by J. M. and
        Margaret Roberts.

1916–1920   Attends and graduates from the Uni-
        versity of North Carolina at Chapel
        Hill. Participates in the Carolina Play-
        makers, directed by Frederich Koch.

1918   Works at Langley Field, Virginia;
        brother Ben Wolfe dies.

1920–1923   Attends Harvard University; studies in
        Professor George Pierce Baker's 47
        Workshop; earns M.A. degree.

1922   W. O. Wolfe dies.

1924   Begins teaching at Washington Square
        College of New York University; con-
        tinues intermittently until 1930.

1924–1925   Travels to Europe for the first time;
            meets Aline Bernstein on the return
            trip.

1926   Abandons plans to be a playwright;
            sails to Europe; begins first novel,
            called at the time *The Building of a
            Wall* (subsequently retitled *Look
            Homeward, Angel*).

1927   Sails to Europe for the late summer.

1928   Sails to Europe in July; Maxwell Per-
            kins at Scribner's accepts Wolfe's first
            novel for publication.

1929   Scribner's publishes *Look Homeward,
            Angel* on October 18.

1930   Begins to experience difficulties in his
            relationship with Aline Bernstein; re-
            ceives Guggenheim Fellowship; sails
            to Europe.

1931   Moves from Manhattan to Brooklyn
            Heights and devotes full time to writ-
            ing.

1935   Sails to Europe; publishes *Of Time and
            the River* and *From Death to Morning*;
            makes first trip to West Coast; speaks
            at University of Colorado Writers' Con-
            ference.

1936   Visits New Orleans; publishes *The
            Story of a Novel*; sails to Europe; at-
            tends Olympic Games in Berlin.

1937   Returns to Asheville for the first time
            since 1929; completes the break with
            Scribner's; signs contract with Harper
            and his new editor, Edward Aswell.

1938   Leaves voluminous manuscript with Aswell; lectures at Purdue University; takes second trip to West Coast, planning to stay in Seattle for several months to write; becomes ill and is hospitalized; is taken by train to Johns Hopkins Hospital in Baltimore; dies on September 15 of tuberculosis of the brain.

1939   Harper publishes *The Web and the Rock.*

1940   Harper publishes *You Can't Go Home Again.*

1941   Harper published *The Hills Beyond.*

1

The Writer from Asheville

A T THE TURN of the century, on October 3, 1900, Thomas Clayton Wolfe was born in Asheville, North Carolina, a resort town nestled in the Blue Ridge Mountains. His father, William Oliver Wolfe, had come from his native Pennsylvania to Raleigh and subsequently to Asheville, where in Pack Square he continued his occupation as a tombstone cutter. (Wolfe's father and the fictional W. O. Gant were always referred to as W. O., initials being an ordinary name designation in the South.) Wolfe's mother, Julia Elizabeth Westall, a native of those mountains, taught school briefly and later became involved with real estate dealings and with her boarding house, the Old Kentucky Home, which she opened in 1906.[1] The marriage of W. O. and Julia, "an epic misalliance,"[2] was stormy. The pleasures derived from bountiful table provisions and happy family gatherings contrasted sharply with the bitter scenes

1

set off by W. O.'s violent drinking bouts and by
Julia's preoccupation with business.[3] Immor-
talized in Wolfe's fiction as W. O. and Eliza
Gant, this couple produced a large family;
Thomas Wolfe was the youngest of the seven
children who survived. Like the parents,
Wolfe's siblings were portrayed in fiction.
Mabel became Helen and Fred was Luke; Frank
was called Steve, Effie was Daisy, and Tom was
Eugene. The twins, Ben and Grover, appeared
in *Look Homeward, Angel* with their actual
names. Thus it was from his own family that
Wolfe drew his strongest and most successful
characters. As letters to family members indicate, these relatives were a source both of life-
long affection and of great difficulty.

Unlike many other Southern writers of the
early twentieth century, Wolfe's ancestors included few teachers, bankers, preachers, or lawyers. He lacked the mark of gentility that often
comes from families who for generations have
handed down aristocratic names, houses, lands,
possessions. The name Wolfe was not a distinguished North Carolina name at that time; indeed, W. O. came from people who spelled the
name "Wolf"; it was he who, for whatever reason, added the final *e*. Perhaps that spelling
seemed to him more distinctive than the
shorter form. Thomas Wolfe's birthplace, the
activities of his family's household, and the
limited ambitions of his brothers and sisters
were "squarely lower middle class,"[4] even
though the Wolfes' income placed them among
Asheville's prosperous citizens. The Wolfes,
however, did not belong to Asheville's elite

society, which included E. W. Grove, whose patent medicines had underwritten the lavish
Grove Park Inn, and George W. Vanderbilt, "who
had modeled the chateau in the midst of his
hundred thousand acres on Blois and Cham-
bord" (Turnbull, 13). The fashionable Grove
Park Inn is still in operation, and Vanderbilt's
Biltmore estate is a popular tourist attraction in
western North Carolina.

Although the Wolfes enjoyed a reasonably
comfortable financial situation, the members
of the household did not share Thomas Wolfe's
intellectual and artistic impulses. Fred Wolfe
did eventually get a degree from what was then
called the Georgia School of Technology, but
Thomas Wolfe was the first of his immediate
family to go off to college and graduate school,
the first to embark on the unheard-of profession—writing. Indeed, to the Wolfe family,
"anyone who displayed intense artistic incli-
nations would have been considered a freak, a
misfit" (Rubin, p. 100). It is true that W. O.—
both in life and in fiction—was a reciter of
verse, but his choices were sentimental favor-
ites and his interest was entertainment, not intellectual engagement. He quoted familiar and
sentimental poems one might find in *One
Hundred and One Famous Poems*, but he
would not have recognized the names of James,
Hardy, or Joyce. Likewise, Mabel was interested
in music, but as Wolfe recorded in *Look Homeward, Angel*, Mabel failed in her dream of becoming an opera star. Instead, her fictional
counterpart, Helen, performed only in the moving picture theaters in small towns such as

Waycross, Georgia. She and her partner Pearl
Hines were billed as "the Dixie Melody Twins."
The Wolfes were, as John Hagan has recently
pointed out, a family of failed artists.[5] And, in
the view of many critics, Thomas Wolfe himself
was also a failed artist.

Certain early events deeply affected
Wolfe's life. In 1904, he and the other younger
children went with their mother to St. Louis,
where she ran a summer boarding house for
tourists at the St. Louis Exposition. Here Grover
contracted typhoid and died; the death was a
severe blow to the family and a decided shock
to Thomas, who was just four years old. Wolfe
movingly recounts Grover's death in *Look
Homeward, Angel* (1929) and tells the tragedy
again in the splendid four-part short story, "The
Lost Boy" (1937). Death was always a central
concern in Wolfe's fiction.

Julia Wolfe kept her youngest son's hair in
long curls and made him sleep with her beyond
a reasonable age; his escape began when, with
his hair finally cut, he entered Asheville's
Orange Street Public School in 1905. The escape
went further in 1912 when he began his four
years at the North State Fitting School, a private
institution in Asheville run by Mr. and Mrs. J.
M. Roberts. In Margaret Roberts Wolfe found
an encouraging and congenial spirit. Even
though her abilities were limited, Margaret
Roberts was a decided influence, a teacher
whom Wolfe revered and who, at a critical period in his life, encouraged his reading and
understood him in a way his family did not and
could not.

His mother, however, was a strong influence also. Julia Wolfe was forty years old when her son Thomas was born, and it seems fairly certain that she knew he would be her last child. She was reluctant for him to grow up and leave her, as if she felt that a great part of life would then be over for her. Her attempt to keep him attached to her is symbolized by her making him move in 1906 to the Old Kentucky Home, her boarding house at 48 Spruce Street. Mabel and W. O. remained at the family house on Woodfin Street, just a few blocks away. Forced to relinquish his place at the table and sometimes even his bed to the boarders, Wolfe was neglected at the same time that he was loved. Julia Wolfe's life was beset with sadness: she suffered many miscarriages and lived to bury not only her husband, but also four of her children—Leslie, Grover, Ben, and Thomas. When John Terry interviewed her in the 1940s, Mrs. Wolfe made several poignant remarks about her children. She said to Terry, "There were so many so near together we did not have the time to give each much attention. We just got used to them and did not have time to appreciate them. This was a fact. We tried to do too much work."[6] The family's relationships were complicated, and certainly Wolfe's relationship with his mother has many sides.*

At sixteen, Wolfe went away to college. Denied his own choices (the University of Vir-

---

* Carole Klein's forthcoming book on mothers and sons will include an examination of the relationship of Wolfe and Julia.

ginia and Princeton), Wolfe acquiesced to W. O.'s preference, the University of North Carolina at Chapel Hill. W. O. assumed that his son would make friends among prominent people of his native state. Such connections would be valuable, W. O. believed, when his son became a lawyer, the profession he had chosen for him. Wolfe's departure for Chapel Hill in 1916 was in a way the final break from home,[7] as the influence of teachers, particularly Frederick Koch,[8] Horace Williams, Edwin Greenlaw, and W. S. Bernard, began to broaden his outlook. His undergraduate career was academically successful; he also edited and wrote for all of the campus publications and held memberships in many important organizations. When he graduated, his list of accomplishments pleased him, but his primary experience from the Chapel Hill years was his participation in the Carolina Playmakers. Frederick Koch, their director, introduced Wolfe "to a writing method that he later used in his significant work"—using material from his own experience (Kennedy, p. 48). Ironically, it was Koch's "undiscriminating encouragement [that] launched him on a writing career that was to become the center of his existence for the rest of his life" (Kennedy, p. 49).

From 1920 to 1923 Wolfe was a student at Harvard, having gone there primarily to study playwriting with Professor George Pierce Baker in his famous 47 Workshop. At Harvard Wolfe was not caught up in campus activities as he had been at Chapel Hill, concentrating instead on his studies and reading voraciously in the Widener Library. Although he received encouragement from Baker and although his play *Welcome to Our City* was produced by the Workshop in 1923, Wolfe could never sell any of his plays to New York producers, and his attempt to become a dramatist failed.

By the end of 1923, Wolfe had completed seven years of college; forced to earn a living, he began teaching at the Washington Square division of New York University, where he was an instructor off and on until 1930. His $150 a month salary did not impress the family, and he admitted to his mother that she probably knew many high school graduates who were doing better than he.[9] Although Wolfe had the chance to go into advertising and eventually received offers to write for Hollywood (the proverbial ways for a writer to get rich fast), he supported himself by teaching and writing fiction.

From 1924 until his death in 1938, Wolfe lived in many different rooms and apartments in Manhattan and Brooklyn Heights. And during these years he went to Europe seven times, his shortest stay being three months. By 1926 he had abandoned his fruitless attempt at drama and started a novel, which at first he called "The Building of a Wall." His fame as a writer came when, after being turned down by numerous publishers, *Look Homeward, Angel* was published by Scribner's on October 18, 1929. While he was alive, Wolfe saw four titles through the press: *Look Homeward, Angel*, in the editing of which he was actively involved; *Of Time and the River*, which was finally sent to the press without his knowledge; *From Death to Morn-*

ing, a collection of short sketches and stories; and *The Story of a Novel*, an expanded version of his 1935 lecture at the University of Colorado Writers' Conference. The posthumous titles, *The Web and the Rock*, *You Can't Go Home Again*, and *The Hills Beyond*, were published from the mountain of manuscript he left and from which he doubtless had planned to shape long novels. What Wolfe left, however, was not finished manuscript material that merely needed editing to be presented as fully conceived novels, although much of this material contains some of his best writing.

Since Wolfe had left Scribner's and joined Harper in 1938, Edward Aswell of Harper was the person who dealt with the voluminous manuscript. Aswell's devotion in bringing out the three posthumous titles cannot be doubted, and his intentions were undeniably good. What Wolfe scholars have always doubted, however, was Aswell's decision to assemble fragments that Wolfe did not live to rewrite and form them into full-length novels. It was Aswell who gave these three books their status, "joined them together, provided transitional passages, and titled them" (Rubin, p. 83). Aswell had help in arranging the material from Maxwell Perkins, Wolfe's former editor at Scribner's, and Elizabeth Nowell, Wolfe's agent. In addition, some of Wolfe's plans for the material were indicated in his own notes and letters. As Wolfe scholars have always known, three of Wolfe's published titles look like books completed by the author but are in actuality the work in great measure of an editor.[10]

The move to New York in 1924 was the final step in Wolfe's leaving his family and the South, which he abandoned by and large as the setting for his fiction after his first novel. In many ways he shared the views of his protagonist George Webber in *The Web and the Rock* that, once removed, the Southerner is ready "to do almost everything, in fact, for dear old Dixie except to return permanently to her to live." Only those who fail and are defeated return, Webber declares—the writer who cannot write, actors who cannot act, painters who cannot paint. While it is true that after 1920 Wolfe never again lived in the South and that after 1929 he hardly visited there, that region was with him always—in Brooklyn Heights, in Munich, in London. Like his fictional displaced Southerners in *The Web and the Rock*, Wolfe was never rid of the South:

It came to them . . . upon the rustling of a leaf at night, in quiet voices on a Southern porch, in a screen door slam and sudden silence, . . . in the memory of the dark, ruined Helen in their blood, in something stricken, lost, and far, and long ago.

No longer a student and not yet a published writer, Wolfe entered this part of his adult life with all the loneliness that had haunted him since his childhood. However, this period also brought his two most important relationships: the love affair with Aline Bernstein and the friendship with Maxwell Perkins. His intense relationship with Mrs. Bernstein was without doubt the most important of all his love affairs.

Perkins was not only Wolfe's editor but also his friend, adviser, and confidant. Eventually, the published speculations that Wolfe could not produce a book without Perkins's help precipitated his leaving Scribner's, a change that was difficult for both editor and author. The importance of their association with each other is reflected in one of Wolfe's last acts. From his hospital bed in Seattle, Wolfe wrote his last letter, a letter that showed he knew how close to death this illness had brought him and that conveyed his deepest feelings. It was to Max Perkins that this letter was written.

Wolfe was returning from his first trip to Europe aboard the *Olympic* when, on September 10, 1925, he met Aline Bernstein. Even though she had not then known Wolfe, she had taken his play, *Welcome to Our City*,[11] with her to Europe for Alice Lewisohn, a Neighborhood Playhouse colleague, to consider. Mrs. Bernstein and Wolfe talked about his future as a playwright, and that discussion "began one of the most publicized love affairs in literary history" (Kennedy, p. 196). Aline Bernstein, a prominent and successful set and costume designer for the New York theater, gave Wolfe entree to the theatrical world. He was not, however, destined to become a playwright, and the meeting with Aline Bernstein ironically ended his quest to enter the theater and soon made possible the writing of Wolfe's first novel. And in Aline Bernstein, Thomas Wolfe found a love that he described in a 1926 letter as "the only comfort, security, and repose I have ever known."[12]

They were, to say the least, an odd pair. Mrs. Bernstein was forty-four, a Jew, petite, northern and city bred, a success professionally.[13] Wolfe was twenty-four, of Presbyterian background, always somewhat anti-Semitic, tall, southern, small-town bred, a frustrated and unpublished writer. Furthermore, Mrs. Bernstein was married to a prominent Wall Street broker and the mother of two children, Theodore Jr. and Edla. With them and her sister Ethel Frankau (who enjoyed a long career as a designer and an executive with Bergdorf-Goodman), Aline Bernstein lived in a large apartment at 250 Park Avenue and in a summer home in Armonk, New York. In his adult life, Wolfe always lived in rented rooms and apartments; the closest he ever came to a happy home life was his years with Mrs. Bernstein. "They were discreet but not furtive. They loved and didn't much care who knew" (Turnbull, p. 105). Yet at best their relationship was made up of a series of extreme emotional swings, and in spite of their initial happiness, their life together was doomed. Years after the affair was over, Aline Bernstein "would say in a pensive moment, . . . that loving Tom was similar to a 'Japanese maiden's self-immolating leap into a volcano: she knew it would be fatal, but she couldn't resist'" (Klein, p. 255).

Their happy days encompassed Wolfe's writing and Aline's designing, his reading to her and her cooking wonderful meals for him. Her financial assistance was given unstintingly, and her encouragement kept Wolfe believing in his talent. The extent of his love for her can perhaps best be seen in two places. In the copy of *Look Homeward, Angel* he presented to her, beneath the printed dedication, "To A. B.," and the epigraph (the fifth stanza of Donne's "A Valediction: Of My Name in the Window"), Wolfe wrote by hand: "To Aline Bernstein: On my 29th birthday, I present her with this first copy of my first book. This book was written because of her and is dedicated to her. At a time when my life seemed desolate and when I had little faith in myself I met her. She brought me friendship, material and spiritual relief and love as I had never had before. I hope therefore that readers of my book will find at least part of it worthy of such a woman" (Klein, p. 240).

The second proof concerns a later work. Near the end of *Of Time and the River*, Eugene Gant and Esther Jack (the fictional counterparts of Wolfe and Aline Bernstein) meet. Of that encounter, Wolfe wrote, "He turned, and saw her then, and so finding her, was lost, and so losing self, was found, and so seeing her, saw for a fading moment only the pleasant image of the woman that perhaps she was, and that life saw. He never knew: he only knew that from that moment his spirit was impaled upon the knife of love." When Wolfe sent Mrs. Bernstein a copy of this 1935 novel their painful separation had long been a fact, but next to this passage he wrote in the margin of her copy the brief message, "Ah, my dear."

Both Thomas Wolfe and Aline Bernstein were talented and strong-willed people, and there were numerous differences in their backgrounds. Eventually, quarrels began and violent scenes followed. On the one hand, Mrs. Bernstein tried too hard to keep Wolfe near her; when he went to Europe, she tried desperately to get his address. Once she had the address, she sent cables and letters declaring her love and longing for his. On the other hand, Wolfe needed to avoid these traumatic disturbances while he tried to work in Europe. His behavior was often reprehensible, however, since he continued to borrow money from Mrs. Bernstein and to seek her advice while still demanding his freedom. In 1932 a particularly unpleasant episode occurred when Mrs. Bernstein came to Wolfe's Brooklyn apartment with a $500 loan. Julia Wolfe was there, and soon after Mrs. Bernstein's arrival the mother and son viciously turned on her and all but pushed her out the door. (When Mrs. Wolfe was interviewed by John Terry in the early 1940s, she recalled this scene in vivid detail.)

Later that year, while she was at Armonk, Mrs. Bernstein failed one day to come downstairs for lunch. Edla found her unconscious and saw several opened vials of sleeping pills nearby. The suicide attempt was nearly successful. Carole Klein points out that close friends felt "that while Aline's depression was certainly real, her attempt at suicide was a dramatic impulse and not a carefully premeditated plan born of the conviction that life would never again be worth living" (p. 292). Wolfe and Aline Bernstein were, as Kennedy describes them, "emotional tinderboxes"; they experienced great love and great despair, which each documented in prose—Wolfe in *The Web and the Rock*, Bern-

stein in *The Journey Down*. Bernstein was older
than Wolfe by nineteen years, yet it was he who
died first. Max Perkins reported Wolfe's imminent death to Mrs. Bernstein and persuaded
her not to go to him at Johns Hopkins Hospital.
Julia Wolfe was there, and no one knew how
she would respond to Aline's presence. Edward
Aswell told Mrs. Bernstein that in his confusion
Wolfe whispered, "Where's Aline. . . . I want
Aline. . . . I want my Jew." And when Aswell
said she was coming, Wolfe "smiled and lay
down again" (Klein, p. 315). Like the marriage
of W. O. and Julia, the affair had been in many
ways an epic misalliance.

Aline Bernstein gave Wolfe financial and moral
support to write his first novel, and she started
it on its journey to publishers by asking her
friend, the critic Ernest Boyd, to read what was
at that stage a giant manuscript entitled *O Lost*.
Not interested in novels, Boyd turned the book
over to his wife, Madeleine, who, although dis-
mayed by its length, finally did read it. Immediately enthusiastic, Madeleine Boyd, as
Wolfe's agent, eventually got the manuscript to
Scribner's and to Maxwell Perkins's attention.
Wolfe was deeply grateful for Madeleine Boyd's
praise and for her efforts, but he had had so
many rejections that the prospect for accep-
tance seemed faint, and in June 1928 he sailed
for Europe. When Perkins expressed serious interest in talking with Wolfe, Mrs. Boyd had to
hire a detective to find him. On October 18,
1928, one year to the day before the publication

of *Look Homeward, Angel*, Madeleine Boyd reported to Perkins that she had located Wolfe in Germany.[14] Once Wolfe got Perkins's letter, he was not sure if the signature was "Perkins" or "Peters" and addressed his dilatory reply to the latter. When at last Wolfe entered Perkins's office, he found that another editor had read his manuscript and had convinced Perkins that it was good. Perkins had carefully read the novel and advised Wolfe that it was to be published. (Later Madeleine Boyd and Wolfe had serious disagreements over royalties. Threats of a lawsuit were made, and finally a settlement was reached in which Wolfe was, characteristically, generous.)

The appearance in 1978 of A. Scott Berg's *Max Perkins: Editor of Genius*[15] provides the fullest account to date of Perkins's role as editor of some of America's finest writers—Ernest Hemingway, F. Scott Fitzgerald, Ring Lardner, and Thomas Wolfe. Perkins's judgments and advice were not infallible, but his authors do bear testimony that his editorial skill was great. Furthermore, Wolfe depended upon his friendship. Scholars have long asserted that Perkins's effort in shaping Wolfe's first novel was probably not more excessive than the editing given most first novels. Years after *Look Homeward, Angel* was published, Perkins recalled that Wolfe "was declined by four or five publishers, but at least two of them had editors who saw that he was a very remarkable writer, and it was only because of what they regarded as the insuperable difficulties of cutting and organizing, etc. and its great length, that it was declined."[16] When dealing with Perkins, Wolfe agreed to the cuts, although later he found it almost impossible to cut.

Perkins, however, did err when, after the success of *Look Homeward, Angel*, he urged that another big book follow. This was the judgment of an editor and publisher, a judgment undoubtedly "injurious to Wolfe's career."[17] At this stage, Wolfe's preference was to publish next "K-19" (the title is taken from the number on the Pullman car that ran from Asheville to New York), and this brief novel got as far as a dust jacket, sales dummy, and opening pages. Although "K-19" was weak and unfinished and clearly should not have been brought out, Perkins's pressure resulted in Wolfe pursuing the long novel. Six years after his first novel, Wolfe finally published his second, *Of Time and the River*, a book that caused a stir in 1935. That year Wolfe lectured at the University of Colorado Writers' Conference, and his subject was the writing and publication process of *Of Time and the River*. Later that year, the lecture appeared in the *Saturday Review of Literature* and prompted a scathing attack from Bernard De Voto. His article, "Genius Is Not Enough," was the catalyst for Wolfe's break with Scribner's. That break, however, was by no means an easy one. Wolfe expressed his anxiety in many letters to Perkins (some never mailed) before he finally left Scribner's and signed up with Harper.

A. Scott Berg discusses the severity of the loss Perkins felt when Wolfe left Scribner's.

Perkins accepted Wolfe's departure with grace, for he believed in its inevitability—"I can easily imagine a biography of Tom written twenty years from now that would ascribe this action to his instinctive and manly determination to free all his bonds and stand up alone," he wrote Marjorie Kinnan Rawlings. . . . But Max already knew that an important part of his life was gone. At the end of the year he wrote Tom Wolfe, "I drink a lonely glass of ale every night in Manny Wolf's while waiting for the paper. . . . We really had a mighty good Christmas, but we missed you." (pp. 335–336)

Richard Kennedy notes that the primary cause for Wolfe's decision to leave Scribner's was his sense that his freedom was restricted there: "For Wolfe to develop as a novelist, it was absolutely necessary that he declare his independence" (p. 337). Wolfe had been an intimate of the Perkins family; he had come to Max with problems ranging from his living arrangements to his dental bills; they were friends as well as editor and author. It was another painful but necessary change in Wolfe's career.

A third important relationship in Wolfe's career was with Elizabeth Nowell, who became his agent after extremely unpleasant circumstances forced him to dismiss Madeleine Boyd. From her sale of Wolfe's story "Boom Town" in 1934 until her own death in 1958, Elizabeth Nowell represented Wolfe competently and faithfully. Theirs was a long-standing association and, although Wolfe sometimes hurt Nowell's feelings, they had mutual respect for each other. An independent and bright woman,

Nowell left her job at *Scribner's Magazine* in 1933 to apprentice as a literary agent with Maxim Lieber, and in 1935 she opened her own agency. Sensitive about the many quarrels Madeleine Boyd had had with Wolfe, Nowell was meticulous in reporting every transaction to him. Indeed, many times she reported to him the sales figures for his work when her commission was less than $5. One of her most difficult times with Wolfe occurred when she had to ask him about her commission on *The Story of a Novel* in book form.[18] Nowell had done considerable work on the manuscript at certain stages and felt she deserved a commission on the book version as well as on the version the *Saturday Review of Literature* published. A good agent and a good businesswoman, she did not enjoy pressing for her commissions, but she often found such action necessary.

Nowell admired Wolfe's work and was offended when Perkins suggested that she lacked enthusiasm for it. Particularly successful in gleaning pieces from Wolfe's morass of manuscript,[19] Nowell sold enough of his work to keep his income adequate. Furthermore, "as time passed, she became, in a sense, a minor Max Perkins to him. Principally, she spurred Wolfe into rewriting episodes as stories" (Kennedy, p. 256). She was highly trusted and respected. After Wolfe left Scribner's, she served as intermediary between Wolfe and Perkins; after Wolfe's death, she edited and published his selected letters and at Perkins's urging undertook the writing of the first biography. Nowell, however, did not see that book through the press:

in August 1958, she died of cancer, and her biography, *Thomas Wolfe*, appeared posthu-
mously in 1960. Bright, energetic, and tough,
she was in many ways an ideal agent for Wolfe;
in every way she was his supporter and friend.

Between 1924 and 1936, Wolfe went to Europe
seven times, spending the greatest amount of
time in England, France, and Germany. Europe
did not hold the fresh, new experiences that
Henry James in *The Aspern Papers* claimed it
did for people of much earlier times; but to a
man like Wolfe, it had glory enough. Although
many of his notebook entries are effusive, neither his European experiences nor his responses
to them were unique. To an extent, he was always a self-conscious American abroad; certainly on his first trip he evinced "all the romantic expectations of a small-town or country
boy who loved books. . . . He made the standard
pilgrimages and visited the literary shrines, and
was, in general, a wide-eyed and romantic tourist" (Holman, *Loneliness*, p. 151). Kennedy and
Reeves suggest that Wolfe's 1930 entries portray him as an "American tourist, alert, sensitive, roaming about and preserving impressions
for future use."[20]
     European travel for Wolfe was filled with
paradoxes. He anticipated each voyage with
great excitement and pleasure, yet notebook entries and letters written during these stays show
him acutely and characteristically homesick
and lonely. As he beheld the wonders of Europe
in art galleries and palaces, cathedrals and museums, great cities and country hamlets, what

he discovered again and again was his homesickness for America. An entry from 1927–1928
headed "Munich" and written in the third person sets down the narrator's view of the traveler. Like so many fictional passages in the
notebooks, this one reflects Wolfe's own attitude toward travel: it was necessary for his
spirit but it also brought disorder. "He realized
suddenly that he did not 'enjoy' travel—it was
a spiritual necessity to him; in some measure
it fulfilled a deep hunger in him for knowledge
and change, and it awoke him from the lethargy
into which he fell after he had been for too long
in one place. But if it renewed him, it brought
with it also incessant struggle, incessant tumult
and disorder" (*Notebooks*, I:191).

Above all, Wolfe never tolerates the idea of
package tours to Europe and satirizes them in
"One of the Girls in Our Party" (1935), a story
that takes a group of middle-western school
teachers to nine countries in thirty-one days.
Untouched by Europe, Miss Blake, the protagonist, spends her time writing mindless letters
back home: "After lunch we saw Trafalgar
Square with Nelson's Monument and the National Gallery. We didn't stay long at the National Gallery, we just stopped long enough to
say we'd seen it." Her inanity contrasts with
Wolfe's deep appreciation for the National Gallery, a place he visited frequently and recom-
mended to American friends, particularly because of a Hogarth painting. By 1928 he had
become a more sophisticated traveler, declaring
in a letter to Aline Bernstein, "I hate to lead the
life of the hotel tourist, who is nursed along

certain main highways like a child, and is told everything by a guide with a memorized spiel in English or French. But I will never succumb to this" (*Notebooks*, I: 221).

Daily schedules and reminders jotted in his notebooks show that Wolfe can be called a real traveler, not a hotel tourist:

Florence. Friday [December 7, 1928] Today—up, left hotel shortly after 10 o'clock—to Cook's—then to the great Uffizi gallery—Stayed 2½ hours—then a trip around town in carriages—above town—and back—First went to Medici chapel—then across river and up hill—then back to grand and gleaming Church of Santa Croce—Then to stone Mosaic works and to leather shop—and back to Cook's—a full and wonderful day. (*Notebooks*, I:268)

Curiously, Wolfe's notebooks and letters rarely refer to his visiting the art museums and galleries in New York and Boston.[21] After his first few years in New York, there are few references even to theater performances, and there is virtually no indication that Wolfe attended musical events in New York. He did hear an opera once with Professor Baker, but he did not frequent the Metropolitan Opera House or Carnegie Hall. (In a 1932 letter to the author Julian Meade, Wolfe wrote that although he lived in New York where he could hear the best music, "I almost never attend a concert or a symphony." Poetry, Wolfe added, filled the place in his life that music filled in the lives of others *Letters*, p. 323). After he turned from drama to fiction writing, it is not surprising that his ardor for the theater cooled. Although he had little interest in music, Wolfe's delight in art was considerable, something he associated with Europe rather than with Boston or New York. In a 1981 paper, Richard S. Kennedy pointed out that in *Of Time and the River* Eugene Gant describes specific paintings he and Francis Starwick saw in the Boston Museum of Fine Art; the paintings were actually ones that Wolfe had seen in Belgian museums.

Wolfe always enjoyed England and France, but his association with Germany was a love affair "intense on both sides, Byronic in its extravagance, like a *blitzkrieg* in its brevity, and a little ludicrous."[22] Hans Schiebelhuth's translation of *Look Homeward, Angel* gave Wolfe an enthusiastic audience, and he enjoyed being lionized in Germany. With sorrow and bitterness he came to recognize the insidious rise of the Nazis and expressed his consternation in "I Have a Thing to Tell You," a short novel *The New Republic* published in three installments in 1937.[23] Because this short novel is so implicitly critical of the Nazis' treatment of the Jews, Wolfe denied himself any chance of returning to Germany, the European country he loved above all others. Any naive enchantment he had fostered was lost in his 1936 visit to Berlin when he finally saw that "the Germany he had loved had fallen to the brown shirts" (Holman, "Wolfe's Berlin," p. 67).

His seven trips to Europe included an idyllic summer month with Aline Bernstein in the English countryside, chance glimpses of James Joyce at a time when Wolfe was too shy to greet him, and conversations with people as diverse as his British publisher and his London char-woman. Much that he did and saw became part of his fiction. What Wolfe assiduously avoided were the American expatriates who left home for residence in Europe, particularly Paris. If by chance he was thrown into their company, he usually insulted them. He did not enjoy F. Scott Fitzgerald and his young Princeton followers, and in *You Can't Go Home Again* Wolfe describes those who fled to Europe as "the pallid half-men of the arts, more desolate and damned than if they had been born with no talent at all, more lacking in their lack, possessing half, than if their lack had been complete." Wolfe's vigor and enthusiasm are always evident. The South of his childhood is never altogether forgotten, but it is displaced by a compulsion to encompass all of America and much of Europe. Wolfe is "the first twentieth-century American writer of major stature who deserts his region to embrace a national and then an international identity" (Holman, *Loneliness*, p. 131).

Thomas Wolfe was a complicated and difficult man, extremely sensitive to the paradoxical pain and pleasure of human relations. In 1927 he wrote bluntly in a letter to his mother that he sometimes thought of his past life—his childhood in particular—"as a man thinks of a dream full of pain, ugliness, misunderstanding, and terror" (*Letters*, p. 119). Yet he did not sever his ties with his family; he faithfully wrote long letters to his mother, Fred, and Mabel; sent them money when he had it; and helped with family trouble if he could. Often family mem-

bers tried his patience, especially in 1935 and
1936 when they frequently called him with exaggerated reports that some of them were in
critical condition; usually the situation was in-
consequential. Rarely did his family realize the
cost a writer pays for interruptions and distress.

Usually in February or early March, Wolfe
sent his mother a birthday greeting, never quite
hitting the exact day, but coming close. He
knew it came in between Lincoln's and Washington's birthdays, which was more than he remembered about anyone else's. Wolfe's letters
to his mother during the 1930s include thank
yous for various gifts she had sent: socks, hand-
kerchiefs, and neckties; fruit cakes; a box of
June apples; grapes, nuts, and raisins; and a
package of good things including an "Easter Egg
which got somewhat crushed in transit" (Letters, p. 288). After Wolfe's death, his mother recalled that he often sent Christmas gifts to the
family, a gesture that suggests close ties. Yet
those ties were sometimes strained.

As we have seen, Wolfe had difficulty in
maintaining professional and social relationships and was often accused of turning against
those who had helped and loved him. Elizabeth
Nowell, who certainly endured Wolfe at his
worst, felt that breaks in such relationships
came because Wolfe was given to excessive hero
worship. The men and women he worshipped
had faults and were after all only human. When
Wolfe found the faults in them, "he felt a bitter
disillusionment, a sense of having been betrayed" (Introduction to Letters, p. xvii). Shy,
defensive, and often suspicious, Wolfe some-

times was also arrogant and, except for brief periods, desperately lonely. In his essay-sketch "God's Lonely Man," he tries to stake out his claim as the mortal who has suffered most from loneliness. As early as 1921, he wrote Professor Horace Williams that "I have tasted to the full this summer the philosophic sweets of solitude but I find it not an unmixed blessing. It is something one enjoys, I think, when one has friends to run from; but when enforced, it loses much of its charm" (*Letters*, p. 18). In 1930 he wrote Max Perkins from Switzerland that "something in me hates being alone like death, and something in me cherishes it: I have always felt that somehow, out of this bitter solitude, some fruit must come" (*Letters*, p. 241). Such sentiments pervade Wolfe's letters, and Richard Kennedy contends that "since Wolfe complained constantly of unhappiness, loneliness, and homesickness, he seems, if he did not enjoy it, at least to have relished telling his correspondents about it," (Kennedy, p. 217). Certainly in the fiction, loneliness is a fact of life for both Eugene Gant and George Webber.

Although Wolfe's social behavior could be charming and proper, he could also drink too much, insult people, and then come around to apologize the next day. Moreover, his innate shyness and self-consciousness were evident when he moved among the wealthy. His letter to Margaret Roberts about a visit to the Rhinebeck, New York, estate of his friend Olin Dows (Joel Pierce in *Of Time and the River*) shows he recognized the problem: "I had to dress up in my dinner jacket almost every night, which was good for me because I'm somewhat afraid of people, and sometimes conceal my fear by being arrogant and sneering magnificently" (*Letters*, p. 124). His biographers, particularly Andrew Turnbull, recount many anecdotes that show Wolfe's worst side. On occasion, his behavior was outrageous. When he was in Europe and trying to escape Aline Bernstein's cables and letters, Wolfe believed that Scott Fitzgerald had betrayed his privacy to Mrs. Bernstein by giving her Wolfe's address. Angry over this intrusion and at the hotel management's decision to charge him extra for bringing in wine from another country, Wolfe went on a rampage: "Told them I was leaving the next day, went on a spree, broke windows, plumbing fixtures, etc. in the town, and came back to the hotel at 1 A.M., pounded on the door of the director and on the doors of two English spinsters, rushed howling with laughter up and down the halls, cursing and singing—in short, *had* to leave" (*Letters*, p. 264). Even more serious was an altercation at the Munich Oktoberfest in 1928, which resulted in a broken nose and deep scalp wounds for Wolfe.

More sedate habits offset this boorishness. For example, it pleased him that he missed only one class during his years of teaching at New York University and that on every student theme he graded he wrote some helpful comment. Much evidence exists in his letters to show that he cared about other people and about their welfare, that he could be and often was generous. But wealthy people and lavish surroundings usually irritated him, that flamboyant style clashing markedly with his own.

Although he was seldom frugal about food and drink, Wolfe paid little attention to his clothes and let dirty shirts and socks pile up alongside crumpled papers. Mrs. Wolfe told John Terry that once Thomas Wolfe came home from Chapel Hill with thirty shirts—all dirty. In a February 18, 1919, letter Wolfe wrote his brother Ben about a hand-me-down suit. (One should remember that by 1918, Wolfe would probably have neared his full six foot, six inch height while Ben was no more than average height.) "I believe you mentioned Christmas that you had an old suit of clothes you were not using. Of course, I wear my uniform on drill days, but Tuesday, Thursday, and Saturday afternoons we have no drill. Most of my stuff is getting frayed except the new suit, so if you don't need this particular suit I would be more than thankful to get it. But please don't send it if you need it at all" (*Letters*, p. 6).

Twenty years later when he made final plans for his speech at Purdue University, Wolfe wrote to Professor Herbert Muller, "My wardrobe at the present time is decidedly threadbare and scanty, but I do have one pretty good blue suit and a tuxedo. I thought I would bring both along, and hope these will meet the sartorial requirements of the occasion acceptably" (*Letters*, p. 744). Indeed, episodes involving clothes often appear in Wolfe's fiction: for example, Eliza makes Eugene wear Ben's castoff shoes, which are several sizes too small (*Look Home-*

ward, Angel); Eugene realizes when he arrives
at the Pierce estate that this visit requires more
changes of wardrobe than his one suit, three
shirts, three pairs of socks, and a change of un-
derwear will allow (*Of Time and the River*); and
Esther Jack struggles to get George Webber
dressed presentably in his new blue suit as he
goes off for the first visit with his editor (*The
Web and the Rock*).

From time to time, Wolfe assured various
correspondents that he was about ready to buy
a house or cottage on the Maine coast or in the
Pennsylvania or North Carolina mountains, but
these plans did not materialize any more than
did his whims about getting married. The only
permanent address he could ever claim was 48
Spruce Street, Asheville, North Carolina, the
address of his mother's boarding house, the Old
Kentucky Home. Whether at 13 East Eighth
Street (a flat with no bath or hot water) or the
Hotel Chelsea, wherever Wolfe lived, his furnishings were meager; he was indifferent to his
surroundings. When he gave up his apartment
at 5 Montague Terrace to go to Europe, he stored
his furniture with the photographer Belinda Jeliffe and her husband. His instructions were casual:

Fixing the chairs etc. is fine, but I don't believe it
would be worth $17 to me to have the chest of draw-
ers fixed. It is a fine piece but I am not a furniture
antiquarian and I don't much care if all the handles
are on or not. What I *would* like to get fixed is my
beautiful and beloved and cigarette-scarred gate-
legged table. Whatever you do will be all right with
me. (*Letters*, p. 469)

However, Wolfe was not oblivious to what household furnishing revealed about character. Esther Jack's Park Avenue apartment, for instance, epitomizes wealth and good taste: "Everything in the house seemed to have been put there to give joy and comfort to people, nothing was there simply as a museum piece to be stared at, everything was in use, and everywhere there was the sense of tranquil dignity, ease, abundance." In contrast to this setting is the pretentious and useless decoration in the house of Joel Pierce's neighbor, Madge Telfair. Inside were "ten thousand little, fragile, costly, lovely and completely useless little things, and their profusion was so great, their arrangement so exquisitely right, their proximity so immediate and overwhelming that one instantly felt cramped, uneasy, and uncomfortable, fearfully apprehensive lest a sudden free and spacious movement should send a thousand rare and terribly costly little things crashing into shattered bits, the treasures of a lifetime irretrievably lost, and one's own life and work and future, irretrievably mortgaged, blighted, wrecked, in one shattering instant of blind ruin."

Although he cared little for the standard possessions most Americans desire, Wolfe was, like his mother, a "pack rat" who saved peculiar things. The catalogue of the William B. Wisdom Collection at Harvard labels several envelopes "miscellaneous," which reveals that the passion for miscellany shown in Wolfe's work derived from his life. He saved dozens of Christmas and birthday cards from Fred, Mabel, the Gambrells (Effie Wolfe's family), and the Westalls, as well as from friends like John Terry, Bob and Marguerite Raynolds, Julian Meade, and Clayton and Kitty Hoagland. One packet contains his English 33 exam and a program of the 1936 Olympic Games in Berlin. There is also a *New Yorker* cartoon picturing a bookstore clerk listening to a female customer ask, "Have you something I can mark time on 'til I'm ready for Thomas Wolfe?"[24] He saved a 1936 permit from the state of Utah to buy liquor, blank stationery from various European hotels, and an FBI circular for an escaped convict with several aliases who was wanted for violating the laws against white slave traffic. He saved invitations (many were written on the backs of calling cards) to cocktail parties, dinners, and picnics. He also saved a curious assortment of business and personal cards, including those from the Sperry Gyroscope Co., Reilly's Bar and Grill, and from Mr. and Mrs. Chester Alan Arthur, Jr. These cards represent a considerable social range and reflect Wolfe's habit of striking up conversations with almost anyone he met. Most people eventually dispose of such items, but Wolfe kept dozens of cards, which survived his moves to different dwellings in Manhattan and Brooklyn. These items give brief glimpses into his daily life and habits.

While Wolfe did not join American expatriates in Europe, he did feel exiled from Asheville after *Look Homeward, Angel* was published. Too many people thought too many family skeletons had been rattled to make going home pleasant. Nevertheless, even though Wolfe's adult life was spent away from the

South, he was by no means totally ignored there or forgotten. In the spring of 1935, Robert Penn Warren, teaching at Louisiana State University, was assembling the first issue of the *Southern Review*, which was to devote space to fiction, poetry, criticism, and articles on social concerns. Warren hoped to secure a manuscript from Wolfe by mentioning other contributors for this issue—John Crowe Ransom, Katherine Anne Porter, Caroline Gordon, Ford Madox Ford, and Allen Tate. Had Wolfe contributed, he would have joined company with the most distinguished writers, and it is significant that in 1935 Warren very much wanted Wolfe included. However, Wolfe sent nothing to the *Southern Review*, probably because he was busy with page proofs for *Of Time and the River* and beset by legal problems involving Madeleine Boyd and later Murdoch Dooher. (Mrs. Boyd sued Wolfe, claiming a percentage of royalties on all his books; Wolfe sued Dooher, who would not return manuscripts Wolfe had unwisely let him offer for sale.)

Other associations with Southern literati came in December 1936 when Wolfe by chance ran into a number of the Vanderbilt University English faculty members who were in Richmond to attend the annual meeting of the Modern Language Association. Wolfe received an invitation from Ransom to lecture, but he refused. At one point, even Faulkner praised Wolfe's great encompassing scheme.[25] During the 1930s, Elizabeth Nowell placed Wolfe's work in many prominent magazines and journals; his good friend Hamilton Basso solicited material from him for *The New Republic*. Thus in the 1930s Wolfe had become a prominent literary figure, and was treated as such when he finally returned to Asheville in 1937. In the early 1930s when the bitterness over *Look Homeward, Angel* was widespread in Asheville, Wolfe certainly would have been rejected there. Indeed, letters of 1936 and 1937 show that even after time had passed, he returned home with reservations. But now he was a world-renowned figure, finally and formally recognized at home.

Wolfe was at a high point in his career when he extended his 1938 western trip and rented an apartment in Seattle, where he planned to settle for several months. However, after a brief trip to Vancouver, Wolfe developed an illness that became increasingly serious. After being treated by doctors he was transferred to Providence Hospital in Seattle, and when his condition worsened alarmingly he was sent by train to Johns Hopkins Hospital in Baltimore, accompanied by his sister Mabel and a nurse, Annie Laurie Crawford. Exploratory surgery revealed tuberculosis of the brain, and Thomas Wolfe died eighteen days before his thirty-eighth birthday.

Had Wolfe lived, he might always have suffered from Faust's impulse to do everything and from Whitman's compulsion to put it all on paper. He wanted to experience everything and to celebrate the length and breadth of America and all the people who make up its cities and towns and countryside. The short novels, the short stories, and *Look Homeward, Angel* represent Wolfe's best work and attest to his technical versatility, his power of observation and portraiture, his telling images, and his lyric prose. His major plan, however, was a series of novels that would span 150 years; that plan was never realized.

That distinguished Southern writer, Flannery O'Connor, expressed a commonly held view of Wolfe when she wrote, "Anybody that admires Thomas Wolfe can be expected to like good fiction only by accident."[26] She admitted that, like many other readers, she had "totally skipped" Wolfe (p. 99). Other readers, as James Atlas implied, get over their enthusiasm for Wolfe, and some even feel apologetic later for having admired him. But by almost any standard, "The Lost Boy," "The Web of Earth," "I Have a Thing to Tell You," "A Portrait of Bascom Hawke," and Look Homeward, Angel are works to admire without apology. Wolfe remains a significant figure of the Southern renaissance. Whatever the flaws in his work, he produced a considerable body of work in which he attempted, with some measure of success, to reveal a great vision.

2

Look Homeward, Angel and *Of Time and the River*
*
"The Apple Tree, the Singing, and the Gold"

W OLFE'S EARLIEST attempts at writing date
from his first trip to Europe in 1924[1] when
he began to record his impressions of fellow passengers and new sights. His November 8, 1924,
letter to George McCoy (a friend who wrote for
the Asheville *Citizen*) accurately describes his
attempts at narrating the voyage and demonstrates Wolfe's shortcomings, some of which
may at this stage be attributed to the exuber-
ance of youth:

I put it all on paper from day to day; I let nothing
escape me, . . . Now that voyage—the poignant emo-

tion of it all, and the astonishing differences in habit
and custom and opinion of different races, English
and American—is recorded hastily, it is true; sometimes clumsily. But it is there. I don't know what
to do with it. I might send it to some American magazine, but it is a conglomerate of so many things—
drama, comment, incident, opinion—that I scarcely
know what to call it. I have given it a title: "A Passage to England." It is written, George, in my own
hand on sheets of white and yellow paper. And my
penmanship is poor.[2]

Few pages of these sketches survive, and
none appeared in a magazine, although one,
"London Tower," was published in the Asheville *Citizen* on Sunday, July 19, 1925.[3] As Kennedy notes, these early sketches are amateurish,
they suffer from weak characterizations, and
they lack the "details of speech, manner, and
gesture—all tricks [Wolfe] later employed to
make his great characters real and memorable"
(p. 99). Nevertheless, by recording these impressions in his notebooks, Wolfe was in a small
way beginning his career.

That career was launched by the publication of *Look Homeward, Angel* on October 18,
1929, the same month in which the stock market crashed. "Perhaps the most autobiographical novel ever written by an American,"[4] the
book had been the center of Wolfe's work since
1926. He reported to Margaret Roberts, "I have
begun work on a book, a novel, to which I may
give the title of 'The Building of a Wall'—perhaps not; because I am a tall man, you know
perhaps my fidelity to walls and secret places"
(*Letters*, p. 111). The novel would go through

many possible titles before the phrase from Milton's "Lycidas" was selected at a late stage. However, the allusion to his "fidelity to walls and secret places" makes its way into the subtitle, *The Story of a Buried Life*.

While almost every character, place, and event in *Look Homeward, Angel* has its real counterpart in the life of Wolfe, his family, their neighbors, and Asheville, the novel most assuredly is about buried lives. The degree to which each member of the Gant family is vulnerable to isolation and to loneliness is extreme. Eliza Gant, for example, never calls her husband anything but "Mr. Gant," a habit not uncommon for a Southern woman of her generation, but a manner of address that is nonetheless extremely formal. W. O. Gant is a wanderer, not a contented husband and father; he finds his consolations in travel and drink, rather than in domestic life. The children are isolated by virtue of their tastes, ambitions, and prospects. While the novel does present the outward actions of this family, it also explores their inner longings and disappointments.

As a family, the Wolfes experienced many frustrations, and to an extent they were hesitant to express deep feelings. They all, in a sense, had "a buried life." In writing *Look Homeward, Angel*, Wolfe was especially indebted to Goethe's *Wilhelm Meister*, Sterne's *Tristram Shandy*, and Joyce's *A Portrait of the Artist as a Young Man*. The freedom from conventional novel form that he saw in these works led him to try similar unconventional forms. All three of these works concern sensitive young men who, like Eugene Gant, come into conflict with their towns, families, and the little worlds about them. Further, they all (as Wolfe said of *Wilhelm Meister*) are concerned with the way these conflicts "illustrate essential elements of . . . man's progress and discovery of life."[5] Wolfe's novel, a bildungsroman, survived its gravest flaws—excessive rhetoric, heavy-handed satire, hyperbole, self-indulgence—and has retained its virtues—lyricism, the effective presentation of the initiations youth must undergo, and the preoccupation with the passage of time and of the loneliness that most of the characters experience. Chronologically, the novel encompasses events in Eugene Gant's life from his precocious childhood to age twenty when he leaves family, Altamont, and the South to move north and enter Harvard. Like young Stephen Dedalus, who abandons his family, Dublin, and the Church, Eugene must break away in order to find himself and to become an artist.

Part 1 of *Look Homeward, Angel* (134 pages) ends when Eugene is almost twelve. Wolfe introduces the reader to the Gant and the Pentland family histories as well as to the young Eugene, who, holding bright wooden alphabet blocks, knows they are "the stones of the temple of language" and strives "to find the key that would draw order and intelligence from this anarchy." The prominent themes introduced in the proem that begins the novel are elaborated in this first part: even as an infant, Eugene realizes that all people are forever strangers, that loneliness is a way of life, and that death comes to young and old. Through the image of the bell, Wolfe introduces Wordsworthian ideas of the soul's preexistence and of the loss and attempted recovery of that prior state of innocence: Eugene "had been sent from one mystery into another: somewhere within or without his consciousness he heard a great bell ringing faintly, as if it sounded undersea, and as he listened, the ghost of memory walked through his mind, and for a moment he felt that he had almost recovered what he had lost." Wolfe's fascination with time pervades this novel; an incident (a sound, a sight, an odor) triggers the memory so that all the past impinges upon and informs the present moment. All of these memories in turn are played out against time immutable, which Wolfe associates with the mountains and rivers.[6] This first part of the novel also emphasizes the pleasure of rituals—the Thanksgiving and Christmas preparations and feasts, W. O.'s building of the winter morning fires, the hearty daily meals, the lush and prodigal harvest from W. O.'s gardens and orchards. Family unity begins to dissipate, however, with the opening of Dixieland, Eliza's boarding house; family concerns now become secondary to her. Instead of gathering regularly as a family group, all the Gants begin to go their separate ways, both in their daily routines and in their spiritual lives.

Part 2 opens with one of Wolfe's best pieces of writing, the nineteen-page chapter that depicts the various activities of Altamont at dawn. Here Wolfe reveals the public and private lives of the inhabitants. Nearly twelve years old, Eu-

gene is finished with many aspects of childhood, and he broadens his experiences intellec-
tually (in the Leonards' private school) and soon
increases his sexual knowledge (on the trip to
Charleston and the encounter with the waitress
Louise). The important characters, Helen, Luke,
Steve, and Ben, are brought to life, especially in
their interaction with Eugene. In another de-
velopment, Wolfe lets Eugene daydream about
idealistic love and heroic rescues of maidens.
(These daydreams are very probably Wolfe's
comic distancing of his own life.) Without denigrating the suffering that Eugene most certainly endures, Wolfe refuses to take that suffering too seriously. In Part 2, the presence of
death once again is important as W. O. enters
Johns Hopkins Hospital to undergo an unsuccessful operation for cancer. And at this point
he begins to die. The aura of death is also prominent because World War I is imminent and because Eugene and Ben are denied their desire to
serve in the army and risk death. At the end of
this part, Eugene is sixteen and, capitulating to
W. O.'s ultimatum, he enters the State University at Pulpit Hill (Chapel Hill).

Part 3 follows Eugene from age sixteen to
twenty, as his range of experience widens. Very
tall and very thin, Eugene's "great raw length
of body, with the bounding scissor legs" make
his movements awkward. And as his college career begins, he declares himself "desperately
lonely." That loneliness continues to be a con-
stant preoccupation for Wolfe about both himself and Eugene. The traumas Eugene undergoes
in this section seem to take a greater toll on him

than the earlier ones. At Pulpit Hill he endures the trials of the greenest freshman and suffers acutely. His sexual initiation is awkwardly completed when he visits a whorehouse in Exeter (Durham) where his more sophisticated friend, Jim Trivett, introduces him to Lily Jones. She observes, "Ain't he the lankiest feller you ever seen? . . . How tall are you son?" Her lovemaking is as impersonal as the sound of her voice: "'Let's git started,' she said. 'Where's my money?'" Eugene's humiliation is intensified by his getting sick the minute he emerges from Lily's house and by his self-consciously asking Jim not to mention this fact. Although Eugene later returns alone to visit the prostitutes, Lily and Thelma, this shabby sexual life results in his contracting venereal disease, not in his embracing romance.

Eugene's life at Pulpit Hill increases the disruption of the Gant family. When he returns for holidays, there is little festive spirit, holidays are gray, and family interest now centers for him almost completely on his taciturn brother Ben. However, in the midst of Dixieland's bleakness comes Eugene's first love affair, the summer romance with Laura James. The brief time that Eugene enjoys the love and attention of Laura is expressed lyrically, reflecting the joy of those moments for him: "Come up into the hills, O my young love. Return! O Lost, and by the wind grieved, ghost, come back again, as first I knew you in the timeless valley, where we shall feel ourselves anew, bedded on magic in the month of June." The interlude of love is short, however. Laura, older than Eu-

gene, returns home to marry her fiancé in Norfolk, leaving Eugene with only a letter of explanation and farewell. His despair is
exacerbated by the boarders' observations:
"'He'll git over it,' said Jake Clapp, in a precise
country drawl, streaked with a note of bawdry.
'Every boy has got to go through the Calf-Love
stage.'" Ben alone understands Eugene's misery.

Part 3 shows how thoroughly the family
members (except Ben) misunderstand and un-
derestimate Eugene and convey these feelings in
bitter words as Eugene nears the final break
with them. Recoiling from Eugene's outburst
toward Luke and her, Eliza whispers, "Unnat-
ural son! You will be punished if there's a just
God in Heaven." Eugene responds with invective:

"Oh, there is! I'm sure there is! . . . Because I have
been punished. By God, I shall spend the rest of my
life getting my heart back, healing and forgetting
every scar you put upon me when I was a child. The
first move I ever made, after the cradle, was to crawl
for the door, and every move I have made since has
been an effort to escape. And now at last I am free,
I am at least locked up in my own prison, but I shall
get me some beauty, I shall get me some order out
of the jungle of my life; I shall find my way out of
it yet, though it take me twenty years more—alone."
    "Alone?" said Eliza, with the old suspicion.
"Where are you going?"
    "Ah," he said, "you were not looking, were you?
I've gone."

This tense scene contains no humor, no hyperbole, no excessive rhetoric. It represents what

is enduring about this novel: Wolfe's ability to convey the deepest emotions in a convincing and compelling manner.

Wolfe's account of Ben's death is equaled only by the poignant account of the death of W. O. in *Of Time and the River*. Ben's death seems the sadder since he died young (at twenty-eight) and never enjoyed full happiness in work or love. As Dr. McGuire says, Ben is drowning from pneumonia; he furiously dismisses his mother from the room with "Get Out! Out! Don't want you." Then he begins humming snatches of old popular songs, ironically "called up now from the secret adyts of his childhood; but always he returned, in his quiet humming voice, to a popular song of wartime—cheap, sentimental, but not tragically moving: 'Just a Baby's Prayer at Twilight.' . . . when lights are low/Poor baby's years/ . . . There's a mother there at twilight/Who's glad to know—." But Ben's mother has been barred from his room. She must hear this song from the other side of a closed door and endure the death of a child she never really knew.[7]

Look Homeward, Angel ends with Eugene talking to Ben's ghost, who advises that only in himself will he find answers to the great questions posed by life. John Hagen has recently argued that Eugene strives to escape from five major constraints—loneliness, family, hometown, native region, and (taken together) time and death. Even though he struggles to escape, he remains "to the end a 'mythmaker,' a visionary, a romancer, an American Adam, who is always seeking to return to the paradise from which he feels he has been expelled."[8] What Eugene (and Wolfe) learns, Hagen concludes, is that "he and the Angel of the title—which has now become his muse—will ultimately 'look homeward' in the broadest sense of all, by immortalizing the family, the town, the region, and his own life in art" (p. 285). And in art Wolfe immortalized them all.

A *cause célèbre, Look Homeward, Angel* brought Wolfe praise from some readers, angry protests from others.[9] The novel has survived for over fifty years even though some critics continue to emphasize its weaknesses.[10] Besides the moments of great emotion and passion the novel conveys, most readers are captivated by the memorable characters that Wolfe presents through their distinctive speech, mannerisms, gestures, and physical details—Ben with his lean, gray face saying beyond reality to *his* angel, "O, my God, . . . Listen to that, won't you"; Eliza, pursing her lips incessantly and declaring about yet another piece of property, "It's a good buy"; W. O., drunk and maudlin, weeping, "Merciful God! . . . it's fearful, it's awful, it's croo-el. What have I ever done that God should punish me like this in my old age"; Luke's stuttering; Helen's nervous laughter; and Grover with his dark, quiet, adult eyes and his strawberry birthmark. In addition to the Gant family, Wolfe presents the entire town of Altamont in vivid minor characters—for example, Horse Hines the undertaker; Hugh Barton's mammoth and dyspeptic mother; and Mrs. Pert, Ben's tipsy lover. There are Altamont's doctors and merchants, its blacks, sum-

mer tourists, natives, and newcomers. Wolfe
views this rich world with candor, often with
compassion, and almost consistently with
humor. In 1930 Wolfe wrote his sister Mabel a
defense of the novel and pointed to some of its
lasting values: "Listen, Mabel: what my book
says in the first paragraph and what it continues
to say on every page to the end is that men are
strangers, that they are lonely and forsaken, that
they are in exile on this earth, that they are
born, live, and die alone. I began to write that
book in London: it is as true of people in London
and Idaho as of people in Asheville" (*Letters*, p.
216).

Of Time and the River was published in
1935; it was also in that year that Pamela Hansford Johnson wrote Wolfe a letter about *Look
Homeward, Angel*, a novel she greatly admired
and that continued to move her. Moreover, her
enthusiasm did not abate (her appreciative
work, *Thomas Wolfe: A Critical Study*, appeared in 1947[11]). Johnson echoed what many
readers and critics said in 1929 and what many
still say: in *Look Homeward, Angel*, Wolfe
spoke for young people who felt that they had
enjoyed and suffered through similar experiences. Johnson had not at this point read the
new novel, *Of Time and the River*, but she implied that she was deferring that reading as one
might delay having dessert.[12] If, as most agree,
Look Homeward, Angel is a novel that speaks
of and to youth, nothing reflects that enthusiasm more than Wolfe's exuberant letter to Margaret Roberts, written in the wave of joy he felt
upon receiving the contract from Scribner's to

publish his first book: "But isn't it glorious that this should have happened to me when I was still young and rapturous enough to be thrilled by it? It may never come again, but I've had the magic—what Euripides calls 'the apple tree, the singing, and the gold'" (*Letters*, p. 166).

Of Time and the River (1935) consists of 912 closely printed pages, an excessive length that Wolfe anticipated when he wrote Max Perkins: "It is going to be a very long book, I am afraid, but there is no way out of it. You can't write the book I want to write in 200 pages" (*Letters*, p. 238). Nearly six years had passed since *Look Homeward, Angel* was published, and many people thought that Wolfe's second novel was long overdue. It was the literary event of 1935 in spite of mixed critical response; however, as Kennedy says, it must truthfully be judged "as one of those magnificent failures that is remembered for its outstanding parts while narrowly conceived successes are forgotten" (p. 272). It is a novel that lacks careful overall structure but whose individual sections are structurally sound.

Of Time and the River continues Eugene Gant's autobiography from age twenty when he enters Harvard to age twenty-five when, returning from Europe, he meets Esther Jack on shipboard. During these years he visits for the first time such places as Boston, New York, London, Paris, Tours, Orléans, and Chartres and is introduced to people and ideas that challenge his thinking. Eugene's introspection continues, and he becomes increasingly aware of both America and the world at large. The framework of travel, however, does not provide a sufficiently tight structure to give the novel unity, and Robert Penn Warren's 1935 assessment was in great measure true: what Wolfe had thus far produced was fine fragments, "really voluminous notes from which a fine novel, or several fine novels, might be written."[13] Years later William Styron echoed these sentiments, saying that in Wolfe's last three novels "many of the great set pieces hold up with their original force" but also finding in them "so much now that palls and irritates."[14] Critics differ about the primary flaws that mar *Of Time and the River*. Holman in *The Loneliness at the Core* sees many scenes "not fully realized because they need to be . . . defined against the controlling thematic pattern" (p. 80), Styron contends that Wolfe "was practically incapable of extended dramatic invention" (p. 105), and Kennedy finds that the "two principal strictures were on the over-emotional egoism of the autobiographical hero and the lack of structure" (p. 273). The novel's flaws have been frequently documented, although many readers have liked it. For instance, Wolfe sent an inscribed copy to Max Perkins's friend Elizabeth Lemmon, who wrote Wolfe that she was ill when the book arrived and thus was uninterrupted in her reading. She noted that parts of the second chapter were so moving that she read them aloud to her sister and on a later occasion read other parts to guests. Lemmon said she had some friends who, like her, were glad to learn that 912 more pages about Eugene Gant existed.[15] And she was right: the book does have appeal.

Whether one calls *Of Time and the River* a fictional thesaurus (Northrop Frye's term) or a literary anthology, no label completely describes this novel that Wolfe labored over for years. It contains a variety of literary forms: dithyrambic chants, catalogues, wordplay exercises, declamations, meditations, parodies, satiric sketches, essays, fantasies, journal notes (Kennedy, p. 271). Certainly this plethora of forms and digressions that often prevent the action from moving does not make up a conventional novel. "Anthology" probably is the best descriptive term for this gigantic work whose effect "is that of a collection of related but disparate entities" (Holman, *Loneliness*, p. 81).

Although Wolfe developed Perkins's suggestion of the search-for-a-father theme, he announced his most pervasive theme in the lyrical line, "of wandering forever and the earth again." In a letter to Perkins on July 17, 1930, Wolfe explained that these two opposing elements are fundamental in people who in one way or another live with a hunger to wander yet still have a great need for permanence (*Letters*, p. 241). This dual theme certainly applies to Eugene, who, like his father before him, becomes a wanderer whose desire for travel is never satisfied. Like Wolfe's, Eugene's longing for permanence is always present as well. The often-repeated words are literally true—"you can't go home again"—and Eugene desires but cannot find permanence in his childhood, his home, his native region. It is only in the brief solace and happiness of love that his restlessness is briefly assuaged. (Indeed, in *Of Time and the River*, love gives Eugene little sense of permanence. By the time Esther Jack fully enters the scene in *The Web and the Rock*, Eugene has metamorphosed into George "Monk" Webber, whose short torso and slightly elongated arms contrast sharply with Eugene's tall, lanky frame.)

Other characters besides Eugene wander in body or in spirit; some, like W. O., relinquish the role of wanderer only when confronted by death. The minor character Francis Starwick, Wolfe's Harvard friend (Kenneth Raisbeck in life), is such a wanderer. He has left his middle-class, provincial, midwestern family, and he now practically denies their existence. It is as if they must be forever remote if he is to flourish as the sensitive aesthete he considers himself to be. His life in Cambridge as Professor Hatcher's assistant is not a permanent existence. When Eugene meets Starwick in Paris much later in the novel, Wolfe presents a sequence of senseless, madcap adventures and wanderings. They are joined by Elinor and Ann, two young Bostonian women who have abandoned their families to follow Starwick in Europe, and the four are almost continually on the move. Night after night they visit the clubs and cabarets of Paris, they dash in and out of restaurants, and they rent cars for side trips that seldom are pleasant. These young people in Paris embody the brittle, phony attitude Wolfe associated with the lost generation. They wander for no purpose, enjoy only the superficial, and (partic-

ularly Starwick and Elinor) play the poseur. The
narrative voice describes Starwick, Elinor, and
Ann as "creatures hopelessly addicted to a drug
. . . [who] could not break the bonds of this tyr-
anny of pleasure which held them. Starwick
seemed to be completely enslaved by this senseless and furious quest, this frantic seeking after
new sensations, this hopeless pursuit of a happiness, a fulfillment, that they never found."
The escapades Eugene indulges in with this trio
bring him little but disillusionment and humiliation. (Elinor frequently exclaims in public
over his flawed French, and near the end of the
sequence she embarrasses him when he asks
that the money he had contributed for their adventures be returned.)

Like Starwick, Elinor, and Ann is the minor
character Robert Weaver, who appears some
half-dozen times in the novel. Whether he
meets up with Eugene in Old Catawba (North
Carolina), Boston, or New York, his hedonistic
living brings disorder. His outrageous behavior
shows his inability to maintain permanence,
and his attempt to win love fails miserably. He
is indeed a wanderer, traveling back and forth
between New York and Colorado to follow the
woman he thinks he loves and reappearing in
Eugene's life sporadically and unexpectedly. In
the Paris trio and in Weaver, Wolfe effectively
portrays the bleak side of the theme. Their ex-
ploits lead them to various places, but none of
these travels fulfills any need or satisfies any
longing. For Eugene, and for Wolfe himself,
wandering was compulsive, but necessary.

Wandering for Eugene brings new lands and new vistas, enriching experiences for the artist.

At first glance, *Of Time and the River* appears to be structured on a mythological foundation. Wolfe divides the novel into eight books: "Orestes: Flight before Fury," "Young Faustus," "Telemachus," "Proteus: The City," "Jason's Voyage," "Antaeus: Earth Again," "Kronos and Rhea: The Dream of Time," and "Faust and Helen." While these mythological and literary associations are not integral to the plot, they suggest a traditional heroic context for Eugene's adventures. However, Wolfe's talent was for portraiture, not the creation of modern myth. He vividly portrays Eugene under the various circumstances and relationships of leaving home, arriving in the city, and discovering Europe, and he depicts Starwick with his small but finely appointed Cambridge apartment, his spectacles with "thick old-fashioned silver rims, and silver handles," his spats and elegant light cane, and his dog named Tang. Other colorful minor characters in the Boston sequence are Professor Hatcher and members of his workshop. Ed Horton is from Iowa, and he and his wife Effie represent common life in contrast to Starwick's refinement. Oswald Ten Eyck, a frail man who gave up his $8,000 job with the Hearst Syndicate to study playwriting, is doomed to failure just as Horton apparently is. Others are briefly but vividly sketched. Hugh Dodd has an earnest stammering eagerness; a man known only as Wood prides himself in officious epigrams—"Barrie is a stick of taffy, floating upon a sea of molasses"; Gray is a young patrician from Philadelphia. Such people are vivid creatures but not suggestive of mythic counterparts.

These minor characters join others from "the great 'art community' of Cambridge and Boston" at Miss Potter's Friday afternoons and dinners. In criticizing this group of failed artists, Wolfe is merciless, calling them "a whole tribe of the feeble, the sterile, the venomous and inept, . . . that museum collection of freaks, embittered aesthetes and envenomed misfits of the arts." Miss Potter is too easily impressed by these misfits and assists in perpetuating their mediocrity by providing them with food and drink. A radically different version of the Bostonian is Bascom Pentland, Eugene's uncle and Wolfe's most interesting eccentric character. Employed in the John T. Brill Realty Company as "Att'y at Law—Conveyancer and Title Expert," Bascom has had a checkered career. As an almost penniless theology student at Harvard (but one who performed brilliantly), Bascom had at one time or another "professed and preached the faith of the Episcopalians, the Presbyterians, the Methodists, the Baptists, and the Unitarians." He does not own a car, will not wear an overcoat in Boston winters (overcoats harbor germs), and strides across city streets with no regard for traffic. Should any motorist assail him, Bascom retaliates by reciting the traffic code of the Commonwealth of Massachusetts on the books since 1856. At this time in his life, he scarcely acknowledges his children and has driven his wife mad. His diet consists of "raw revolting messes of chopped-up carrots, onions, turnips, even raw potatoes, which he devoured at table, smacking his lips with an air of keen relish, and declaring to his wife: 'You may poison *yourself* on your old roasts and oysters and turkeys if you please: you wouldn't catch *me* eating that stuff. No, sir!'"

Scattered among the musty law books in Bascom's office are the poems of Matthew Arnold, the essays of Ralph Waldo Emerson (Wolfe describes Bascom as "the great Ralph Waldo Emerson with the brakes off"), and "the *Iliad* in Greek with minute yellowed notations in the margins." Now this former student of Greek is reduced to criticizing Brill's suggestive stories and obliging his employer by using big words to impress the clients.

Bascom functions symbolically as age, in contrast to Eugene's youth. In addition, in this northern city far from home, Eugene finds in Bascom a link with the past. And in this minor character Wolfe explores another example of the buried life: "And now, as the boy looked at the old man, he had a sense of union with the past, the voices of lost men, the pain, the pride, the madness and despair, the million scenes and faces of the buried life—all that an old man ever knew—would be revealed to him, would be delivered to him like a priceless treasure, as an inheritance which old men owed to young, and which should be the end and effort of all living."

When Wolfe returns the novel to Altamont, excellent characterization continues. He gives a detailed portrayal of Hugh McGuire (the doctor who keeps W. O. alive so long), who spends

long nights in his hospital office drinking corn
liquor from a jug at his feet while he reads letters the woman he loves has written to another
man. But in the end McGuire cannot save Gant.
Wasted by cancer, the old man awaits death as
his wife sits by, watches, and sees to his needs.
The reader, who has witnessed W. O.'s escapades and who remembers the disruptive path
his marriage and family life have followed, is
nevertheless deeply touched by his words at the
end: "'Eliza,'—he said—and at the sound of
that unaccustomed word, a name he had spoken
only twice in forty years—her white face and
her worn brown eyes turned toward him with
the quick and startled look of an animal—
'Eliza,' he said quietly, 'you have had a hard life
with me, a hard time, I want to tell you that I
am sorry.'" Eliza's response consists of a few
broken words, and the narrative voice reveals
her true emotion: "And suddenly these few simple words of regret and affection did what all
the violence, abuse, drunkenness and injury of
forty years had failed to do. . . . Digging her fist
into her closed eye quickly with the pathetic
gesture of a child, she lowered her head and
wept bitterly." Such a scene shows Wolfe at his
best, not only portraying convincing characters
but also conveying emotion that goes to the
heart.

Quite a different character portrait is that
of the Simpson family, whose daughter Genevieve is courted by Eugene. However, Eugene's
interest is not really in the daughter but in discovering the family secret. During one visit he
manipulates the conversation so that the young

son Jimmy blurts out the truth about the missing father: "Sure, . . . he's livin' with another woman." Delighted in having exposed the family skeleton, Eugene faces the consequences of his actions when Mrs. Simpson asks his intentions toward Genevieve and Eugene replies that he has none. Wolfe gives Mrs. Simpson all the dignity a character needs when she replies, "All right, . . . That is all I wanted to know. . . . I don't know why you thought it was such a joke, but I think you will live to see the day when you are sorry for it. It's not good to make a joke of people who have liked you and tried to be your friends." Although this episode is brief, the mystery of a family secret anticipates the longer and more involved episode of the Coulsons,[16] the English family who rents Eugene a room. Their private lives hold mysteries that Eugene never solves; their family secrets are apparently shameful, and these secrets remain undisclosed.

In the section "Proteus: The City," Eugene begins his teaching career. Among his predominantly Jewish students is Abraham Jones, who, with his family, is another interesting minor character. Wolfe devotes nearly one hundred pages to another phase of Eugene's life, his friendship with Joel Pierce and his family, who live on their Hudson River estate. In particular, Wolfe recounts the night the hopeful young Eugene reads his play aloud to Joel and his sister whose attention and praise contrast sharply with the relative indifference of his own family. Memorable details are also given of Eugene's fellow occupants of New York's Hotel Leopold, and although Mrs. Grey, Mrs. Martin, Doctor

Withers, Mrs. Buckles, and Doctor Thornton play only minor roles, Wolfe makes them credible characters.

Once in Europe, Eugene finds innumerable people to meet, ignore, or retreat from. In the "Jason's Voyage" section Wolfe introduces not only the Coulson family (who live outside of Oxford) and their boarders (auto workers who play frantic jazz every night) but also the Rhodes scholars (Johnny, Price, Fried, Sterling) who irritate Eugene with their pretensions yet simultaneously arouse his envy. In Paris there are Elinor, Ann, and Starwick; in Orléans there is the incredible and outrageous Countess de Caux, a guest at the Grand Hotel du Monde d'Orléans, who, when Eugene mentions that he is a writer, jumps to conclusions that suit her schemes. Immediately she declares that Eugene writes for *The New York Times* and soon amends her story to make him the editor. She babbles on about knowing rich Americans and announces that her diet consists entirely of horse's blood. Her absurd schemes reach their climax when, because she has so successfully misrepresented the young American writer, she receives a luncheon invitation for them both. Their hostess, La Marquise de Mornage, believes that Eugene knew her son "Paul when he visited American with Le Marechal Foch in 1922." Eugene's furious refusals do not suffice to deny the Countess this social honor (her last visit to Mornage was seven years before), and the final grotesque episode occurs: Eugene, who had dreaded the Countess's outrageous plot, is nevertheless "stirred by a profound, tranquil

and lovely joy at the noble beauty and simplic-
ity of the chateau." These feelings are inter-
rupted by the revelation that the countess is not
on a strict diet at all but is instead a poor,
starved woman. She looks at the table with hys-
terical delight and eats

like a famished wolf. . . . Her sharp and greedy little
eyes glittered with an almost delirious joy, she
would seize a glass of wine and drain it in one greedy
gulp; at times she was so excited by the variety and
abundance of the dishes that she seemed unable to
decide what to reach for next. She reached out greed-
ily in all directions, her eyes darting avaricious
glances to and fro, chicken, meat, vegetables, salad,
wine disappeared as if by magic, and were replen-
ished, and all the time the poor old woman chuckled
craftily to herself.

Wolfe never reveals the Countess's full
story. We never know what caused her penu-
rious condition or why she is given to such extravagant claims about people of whom she
knows nothing. But when Eugene returns almost penniless to Orléans from Tours, he tries
to play the Countess's game on her, saying he
has reported far and wide how she helps and
befriends Americans. When he asks her to stand
credit for four or five weeks at the hotel, she
answers simply, "I have not got it." The best
she can do is confer in an excited voice with the
hotel officials and return to Eugene with a ten-
franc note, barely enough for a third-class railway ticket to Paris. The scene in which he had
planned to turn the tables on her is finally one
of discomfort for them both:

He had been surprised and disappointed at the meagre exactness of her loan: he had eaten nothing all day long and suddenly, with no funds to spare and the prospect of a continued and indefinite fast before him, he felt ravenously hungry. And now it was his turn to redden with embarrassment; he found it difficult to speak, and in a moment said hesistantly:

"I wonder if these people would let me have a sandwich. . . . I've had nothing to eat."

She did not answer; he saw the faint flush deepen on her sallow cheeks again and, already sorry for the additional distress his request had caused, he said quickly,

"No, it doesn't matter. I'll get something when I get to Paris."

It is in the rendering of such portraits, in the bringing to full life of even such minor characters as the Countess, that Wolfe's greatest strength as a writer lies. Any reader of *Look Homeward, Angel* remembers W. O. and Eliza, Helen and Luke and Eugene. But many readers of Wolfe's novels can also recite a list of memorable minor characters.

Wolfe's hauntingly beautiful lyrical passages also add to the success of his style. Although some are too long, others are moving and effective. While these passages may not advance the plot, they provide moments of reflection and meditation, just as arias in an opera provide introspection. The "Telemachus" section, for example, opens with W. O. Gant dead, and as Eugene lies in a bed in his mother's house, the narrative voice ruminates on the month of October and on the bittersweet emotions that come with the fall of the year and with death. Wolfe imagines October in Virginia, Maine, the Palisades, Ohio, Pennsylvania, and throughout America. His Whitmanesque sweep and penchant for the catalogue are especially effective in these seven pages. In almost every paragraph, concrete details have been carefully selected as Wolfe characterizes a month of the year. Even a brief sampling illustrates his seemingly inexhaustible responses to October and the chain of association the month holds demonstrates his poetic force.

October is the season for returning: the bowels of youth are yearning with lost love. Their mouths are dry and bitter with desire: their hearts are torn with the thorns of spring. For lovely April, cruel and flowerful, will tear them with sharp joy and wordless lust. Spring has no language but a cry; but crueller than April is the asp of time.

All things on earth point home in old October: sailors to sea, travellers to walls and fences, hunters to field and hollow and the long voice of the hounds, the lover to the love he has forsaken—all things that live upon this earth return, return: Father, will you not, too, come back again?

This lyric passage from the "Telemachus" section of *Of Time and the River* closes with a recognition of the permanence of loss and death. No pleading for return and relief will be answered; nothing from the past can be restored. "He knew then that his father would not come again, and that all the life that he had known was now lost and broken as a dream."

Yet another of the lyric passages opens the "Kronos and Rhea" section, in which Wolfe catalogues various scenes that occurred in different centuries. The motif, "Play us a tune on an unbroken spinet," introduces Mozart playing in a parlor. The scenes that follow show Athens on an average day, poor people sitting in their rooms and a rich man sitting with his back to the fire in the middle ages, Tobias Smollett passing the window, and voices throughout America, where people lead lives "more dark and strange than the lives of the Saxon thanes." Wolfe continues this indulgence in his dream of time, the last part of this section, which ranges across centuries and continents and ends with Eugene's persistent cry, "Father, I know that you love, though I have never found you." This cry again emphasizes Wolfe's innumerable debts to Joyce, since it echoes Stephen Dedalus's search for the father in *Ulysses*.

These two examples of Wolfe's lyric passages demonstrate the poetry of his language. Nevertheless, even the best of these passages sometimes go on too long, and their genuine emotion can easily dissolve into bathos.[17] When Eugene becomes homesick in Tours, the narrative voice hyberbolically declares that he is homesick for "a million memories, ten thousand sights and sounds and shapes and smells and names of things that only we can know." And Wolfe catalogues battles, wildernesses, states, Indian nations, railroads, notorious tramps, and mighty rivers. While this passage once again presents the ironic position Eugene finds himself in—delighted in a foreign land but homesick for America—and while the details themselves are good, the sheer amount of information is overwhelming.

Wolfe kept Joyce's *Ulysses* near him and derived many ideas and much pleasure from it.[18] Long before he had published anything and while sections of *Ulysses* were just appearing in the *Little Review*, Virginia Woolf wrote her essay "Modern Fiction" (1919). She took Wells, Bennett, and Galsworthy to task for spending "immense skill and immense industry making the trivial and the transitory appear the true and the enduring."[19] Her praise for Joyce was profound and her judgment about the new direction the novel was taking is still sound:

Any method is right, every method is right, that expresses what we wish to express, if we are writers; that brings us closer to the novelist's intention if we are readers. This method has the merit of bringing us closer to what we were prepared to call life itself; did not the reading of *Ulysses* suggest how much of life is excluded or ignored, and did it not come with a shock to open *Tristram Shandy* or even *Pendennis* and be by them convinced that there are not only other aspects of life, but more important ones in the bargain? (p. 124)

Virginia Woolf's defense of the author's necessary freedom of method may not excuse a writer like Wolfe for his excesses, but it may justify his attempt, as he expressed it, "to get everything down on paper."

Although Wolfe treats time in many ways throughout *Of Time and the River*, one of the most effective meditations, and one of the finest scenes in the entire novel, is the "Ces arbres" passage in the "Kronos and Rhea" section. Eugene is in a French sidewalk cafe. The waiter, wearily piling up the chairs, puzzles over this late customer who keeps muttering, "Ces arbres . . . ces arbres. J'ai—J'ai—Mais je les ai vu avant— . . . J'ai dit que—ces arbres—je le les ai vu." When Eugene finally realizes that the waiter does not understand his words at all, he leaves. What had so perplexed him was his having looked from the cafe chair to the scene in front of him—the great wreathed branches of trees that blended into a memory that would not surface—and trying to discover the meaning he knew was there:

And suddenly, with a thrill of recognition that flashed across his brain like an electric spark, he saw that he was looking at the same trees that Van Gogh had painted in his picture of the roadmenders at their work in Arles, that the scene was the same, that he was sitting where the painter had sat before. And he noted that the trees had tall, straight, symmetrical trunks, and remembered that the trees that Vincent had painted had great, tendoned trunks that writhed and twisted like creatures in a dream— . . . so that now he could not forget them, nor see this scene in any other way than that in which Van Gogh had painted it.

Wolfe is successful in conveying the details of van Gogh's painting *The Roadmenders*, and he also succeeds in linking different periods of time. Present time (Eugene in the cafe) links with past time (when Van Gogh painted these trees). That memory triggers Eugene's memory and calls up "unfathomed memories of home, and . . . something in his heart he could not utter." That which lies too deep for words is time immutable, that time of great mountains and rivers. This long and unconventional novel has many memorable parts. *Of Time and the River* still finds readers who will argue that it is, if nothing else, a book of magnificent fragments.

3

The Web and the Rock and *You Can't Go Home Again*
*
Novels of Magnificent Fragments

IN HIS DISCUSSION of Wolfe's Webber novels (*The Web and the Rock* and *You Can't Go Home Again*), Bruce R. McElderry gives good advice: "With Wolfe, more than with most authors, the reader must tolerate some rough roads and some detours if he is to enjoy the best scenery."[1] These novels share most of the faults and some of the virtues of Wolfe's earlier works. Both of course are posthumous works fashioned by Edward Aswell from the voluminous material Wolfe left at his death; furthermore, he had written some of this material as early as 1930.

When Wolfe returned from lecturing at the

1935 University of Colorado Writers' Conference and the extended trip he took farther west
after the conference, he had gained an expanded
view of America, a greater understanding of his
own country that would be reflected in his
work. In 1935 he published *Of Time and the
River* (March 8) and *From Death to Morning*
(November 14); *The Story of a Novel* (Wolfe's
explanation of his difficulties in writing *Of
Time and the River*) was published in book form
on April 21, 1936. With four titles in print,
Wolfe now engaged in three overlapping projects: the continuation of the six-volume series
whose titles were announced in the prefatory
pages of *Of Time and the River*; a book about
nighttime in America ("The Hound of Darkness"); and an attempt at objective narration
("The Vision of Spangler's Paul").[2] In trying to
write of Paul Spangler rather than Eugene Gant,
Wolfe tried to silence some of his critics'
charges, particularly the frequent charge that
his fiction was too autobiographical. Although
notebook entries, portions of letters, and early
drafts of sections for novels include the names
of Paul Spangler and Joe Doaks, neither survives
as a character in Wolfe's novels. Instead, the
name of Wolfe's new protagonist became
George Webber, and although he is in essence
Eugene Gant–Thomas Wolfe, he has a radically
different childhood and bears no physical resemblance to Eugene.

The table of contents for *The Web and the
Rock*, even more elaborate than that for *Of
Time and the River*, lists the titles of eight
books that in turn contain fifty chapters, all

with titles. The novel falls into two parts: Books I–III (293 pages) cover George Webber's childhood in Libya Hill, his years at Pine Rock College, and his move to Manhattan. Books IV–VIII (400 pages) cover the tempestuous love affair of Esther Jack and George Webber as well as Webber's unsuccessful attempts at publishing his first novel, *Home to Our Mountains*. In this second part, Wolfe returns to autobiographical material in earnest. Like *Look Homeward, Angel, The Web and the Rock* begins with family history; Wolfe introduces John Webber, who marries Amelia Joyner in 1885. Their son George is born in 1900, the year of Eugene Gant's birth. Like W. O. Gant, John Webber comes from Pennsylvania and works with his hands. (He is a builder who insists on using brick rather than the traditional wood.) As with Eliza, Amelia Joyner's people come from the hills, and remnants of the Joyner clan move into town after the Civil War.

John Webber and Amelia have only one child, and in 1908, after some twenty years of marriage, John, in his sixties, causes a scandal by leaving his wife for "a young woman married to a man named Bartlett." His behavior is considered unseemly, but he lives with this woman until he dies in 1916. A stylish dresser (somewhat resembling W. O. Gant), Webber wears a well-cut black broadcloth suit, starched cuffs, wing collar with a cravat of black silk, and a pearl gray hat—the symbols of propriety. Like Gant, John Webber drinks, and of that weakness Amelia's father had declared he "would rather see a daughter of mine dead and lying in her

coffin than married to a man who drank." Like
Gant, Webber had had an earlier marriage that
ended in divorce at a time when people like
Amelia's father agreed that "murder could have
been—and was—far more easily forgiven than
divorce." John Webber, however, bears no physical resemblance to Gant, and Wolfe's imagery
makes him more animal-like than human. In
spite of his above-average height, Webber gives
the appearance of being shorter than he is. His
body is bowed, his legs short, his shoulders
burly. Since George Webber is his father's dou-
ble, it is not surprising that his nickname is
Monkey, often shortened to Monk.

When Amelia dies shortly after the scandal
breaks, George Webber is taken by the Joyner
kin to grow up in the one-story frame house his
grandfather had built forty years ago. The small
house is "obscured and dwarfed by its more
splendid neighbor," that of Monk's uncle, Mark
Joyner, and his wife, Mag, a pious Baptist.
Raised primarily by Aunt Maw, the Joyners'
old-maid sister, Monk somehow maintains a
sunny disposition in spite of a dark and mel-
ancholy childhood. The chronicle of his father's
sinful and godless life is told again and again,
usually by Aunt Maw, who is a gloomy woman.
Her sour ways and unending calls for Monk to
go to work elicit a flagrantly antifeminist passage, a frequent occurrence in Wolfe's writing.
Even though the passage comes from the child's
point of view, it is still a denigrating view of
women. What George resents is not the work
but what Aunt Maw symbolizes:

It is that women in the early afternoon are dull, and dully ask dull things of us; it is that women in the afternoon are dull, and ask us always for a little thing, and do not understand! It is that at this hour we do not want them near us—we would be alone. They smell of kitchen steam and drabness at this time of day: the depressing moistures of defunctive greens, left-over cabbage, lukewarm boilings, and the dinner scraps. An atmosphere of sudsy water now pervades them; their hands drip rinsings and their lives are gray.

Here Wolfe attributes a smallness and meanness of spirit to women and their restrictive domestic lives. These traits are present in Aunt Maw—and in many other women characters—who is a convenient target. Rarely does Wolfe portray important male characters in such a way. Furthermore, this passage serves to show the bleak existence of the boy George Webber. The Gants had their shortcomings to be sure, but at least there were brothers and sisters, abundant gardens, and roaring winter fires.

George Webber escapes from this drab existence by thinking of the freedom, romance, and order he associates with his absent father. Also, from his earliest recollections, he has "the sense of the overpowering immanence of the golden life." Although he has no explicit vocabulary for this feeling, "he had a thousand spells and prayers and images that would give it coherence, shape, and meanings." Sustained by this inner and private life, George also finds comfort in his older friend Nebraska Crane, one of Wolfe's most interesting minor characters,

and in his dream of the golden city and the freedom it promises.

Much of George's childhood is touched by
threats of harm and by actual violence. Such a
threat is implicit in the episode about eight
black boys riding their bicycles and taunting
George, gleefully insisting that his name is
Paul:

"How's ole Paul today?"
"My name," the boy said firmly, "is not Paul! My
name is George!"
"Oh, no, . . . " cried the black boys, grinning ami-
ably. "Yo' name is *Paul*!"

George's frustration is all the more agonizing
because he faces the eight alone, and they will
not listen to his protests or stop their irksome
cries. Far more disturbing is the behavior of
Mag's nephew Tad (one of two nephews living
in the big brick house of Mark Joyner), who
brings to his attic laboratory "small, panting
birds, vibrating cats, stray curs—noting with
minute curiosity their sensory responses when
he drove pins into their eyes, cut off portions
of their tails, or seared them with a heated
poker." His aunt's reaction is as shocking as
Tad's sadistic behavior: "That boy's a born nat-
uralist." Although Wolfe presents no episodes
involving George with Tad, the radically different cousins do live in adjacent houses. Another difficulty is Mark Joyner, a curious man
in whom parsimony and generosity war. He harbors "a hidden volcano of anger" that from time
to time is so near eruption he must leave his

household and walk in the woods for hours until calm returns.

A different kind of terror for George is the accident of his friends, Albert and Johnny Andrews. As their yellow wagon with "Leader" painted on the side comes down the street, it is hit by an Oldsmobile driven by young Hank Bass. The horror of the scene is intensified by the arrival of the boys' mother, looking like a demented hag, and their father, grotesquely shaped from a disease of the joints. The adopted son, Johnny, survives; Albert does not. "And Monk was sick to his guts because Albert had shouted at him and been happy just a minute ago, and something immense and merciless that no one understood had fallen from the sky upon him and broken his back and no one could save him now." Almost immediately after this episode of horror, Wolfe recounts another violent wreck on the same corner, but this one is a parody of the earlier tragedy. Lon Pitcher, his 1910 Cadillac loaded with chorus girls, is being chased by the policeman, Mr. Matthews. Pitcher, who is as drunk as he can be, wraps the car around a telephone pole, yet all of the car's occupants are unharmed. The irony of fate lets this insensitive group walk away from an accident on the very corner where the Andrews child was killed. And, as Wolfe implies, there is no explanation for the result of life's accidents.

Chapters 7 and 8 in Book II continue this unrelenting violence. In the chapter entitled "The Butcher," Wolfe presents the strange Lampley family. A butcher by trade, Mr. Lampley came to Libya Hil twenty years ago but has always remained a stranger. His brutal profession is reflected in his physical traits: a small red face that displays "the choleric and glaring color of the Irish," a hideous scar that draws and twists his face to one side, and unwinking eyes that stop anyone's overture of friendship. His wife, the largest woman George has ever seen, epitomizes coarseness. Her stories are unsavory, yet she chokes with laughter when she tells them. Their two children have turned out badly. Baxter, the son, steals from his boss and is forced to join the navy to avoid further trouble. When he leaves, his father threatens to kill him if he ever returns. The daughter, Grace, is fifteen, and her vacant smile and innate sensuality suggest her future. Soon her involvement with Jack Cashman rouses her mother's suspicions. Wolfe dehumanizes Mrs. Lampley completely, writing a violent passage rarely surpassed in his fiction:

"Well," said Mrs. Lampley slowly, as she stared ahead, "I took her down into the cellar—and," she said with virtuous accents of slight regret, "I don't suppose I should have done it to her, but I was so worried, so worried," she cried strangely, "to think that after all the bringin' up she's had, an' all the trouble me an' Lampley had taken tryin' to keep her straight—that I reckon I went almost crazy. . . . I reached down an' tore loose a board in an old packin' case we had down there," she said slowly, "an' I beat her! I *beat* her," she cried powerfully, "until the blood soaked through her dress an' run down on the floor. . . . I beat her till she couldn't stand," cried Mrs. Lampley, with an accent of strange maternal virtue in her voice.

The passage continues. The disparity between the woman's deeds and the tone in which she relates them—"virtuous accents of slight regret," and "an accent of strange maternal virtue"—underscores the horror.

Sheer violence is a force in most of Wolfe's fiction. It is a disturbing presence epitomized in his story "The Child by Tiger," which is based on a man named Will Harris (alias James Harvey), a mysterious black man who came to Asheville in November 1906 and bought clothing and a secondhand rifle. On November 13 he went on a rampage that left five citizens dead (Kennedy, p. 316). Wolfe transformed the incident into a short story of some 10,000 words, which Richard Kennedy calls the outstanding short story of Wolfe's career (p. 315). The fictional black man, Dick Prosser, having served a long enlistment in the army with a crack troop of blacks on the Texas border, comes finally to Libya Hill, works at odd jobs, and lives in a white-washed basement room at the Sheppertons' house. More like a monastic cell than a rented room, his living quarters reflect order, quiet, and deeply religious habits. But one winter night, Dick Prosser goes berserk. The savagery begins in Pansy Harris's shack in Niggertown; when it ends Prosser has shot six men, five of whom die. Men gather, arm themselves, and go after Prosser. In the end, he stops running at the creek, calmly sits on the bank, removes his shoes, and faces his pursuers.

Wolfe's account of Prosser's death is reportorial and objective, lacking his usual rhetorical flourishes. Terse, swift, and suspenseful, the narrative moves to its climax:

The men on horseback reached him first. They rode up around him and discharged their guns into him. He fell forward in the snow, riddled with bullets. The men dismounted, turned him over on his back, and all the other men came in and riddled him. They took his lifeless body, put a rope around his neck, and hung him to a tree. Then the mob exhausted all their ammunition on the riddled carcass.

Prosser's body is publicly displayed in the undertaker's window, where all the town, driven by innate fascination for the gruesome, protest and shudder and declare they "will not go. But in the end they always have their look." A brief coda is set years later as the narrator remembers Prosser's neat room, the ringing of the town's alarm at 2:00 A.M., the heavy snow, Prosser's violence, and the mob. Wolfe then quotes "Tiger! Tiger!" finding in Blake's meditation upon the mysterious source of evil and violence the answers to the riddle posed by Prosser's story. "Men debated and discussed these things a thousand times—who and what he had been, what he had done, where he had come from— and all of it came to nothing. No one knew the answer."

"The Child by Tiger" episode functions as a pivotal experience in George Webber's childhood and survives well as a short story[3] independent of its appearance in *The Web and the Rock*. As Monk Webber grows up, attends Pine Rock College, and finally goes to New York, Wolfe introduces several important minor characters: the absurd "Major" Joyner, who is Bascom Pentland made over; Jerry Alsop, the col-

lege pseudo-intellectual; and Jim Randolph, the
football hero who never gets over his years as
the athlete-idol. The theme "of wandering and
the earth again" is reintroduced, and when
Monk arrives in New York, that golden city of
promise, Wolfe emphasizes youth's great expectations: Monk thinks that because he is
young and full of glory, he can never die. However, disillusionment quickly sets in, and reciting past successes brings no happiness. The college friends who have lived together now go
their separate ways, and Wolfe has Monk confront loneliness, that familiar Wolfe theme.
Monk must face the fact that "all were gone at
last, one by one, each swept into the mighty
flood tide of the city's life, there to prove, to
test, to find, to lose himself, as each man
must—alone."

The second half of *The Web and the Rock*
parallels the facts of Wolfe's meeting Aline
Bernstein on board ship when he returned from
Europe, their love affair and subsequent
breakup, his teaching at a branch of New York
University, and his frustrating early attempts to
publish *Look Homeward, Angel*. Thus this second part returns to autobiographical material as
its source to a far greater degree than the first
part of the novel. Although *The Web and the
Rock* gains some unity when it is juxtaposed
with *You Can't Go Home Again*, it remains, as
Herbert Muller points out, "an unsatisfying
novel: a whole which is not greater than the
sum of its parts, in which the best parts do not
gain by their relation to the whole."[4]

Probably so. But still the second half very

convincingly portrays two people in love. Esther is much older than George and possesses fame, wealth, and connections; George has the pomposity that comes with youth, a slim income, and is as yet an unknown writer. Esther Jack's house is tasteful and comfortable, reflecting all her good qualities. She entertains well, gives successful parties, and moves with ease among her fellow celebrities. Without Esther's touch, George's living quarters are drab and disorderly, a "pell-mell circle of books, shirts, collars, neckties, socks, stained coffee cups half filled with sodden butts, post cards, letters five years old and laundry bills, student themes and tottering piles of his own manuscript, notebooks, a ragged hat . . . a cyclonic compost of the dust and lumber of the last ten years."

But the early period of their relationship is ideal. Characteristically, Esther is excited about her work, flushed with energy, charged with gaiety. She brings to George, as the title of Chapter 24 suggests, "A New World." In the upstairs apartment they share, they pursue their separate work. Occasionally, Esther recounts episodes of her childhood for George or relates the details of her working day at the theater. On many evenings Esther cooks irresistible dishes for George.

The narration of their love affair begins in Chapter 21, when George meets Esther on the steps of the New York Public Library and they go off joyously to celebrate his twenty-fifth birthday. By Chapter 30, "The Ring and the Book," Esther's fits of jealousy are countered by George's harsh retorts and sarcastic remarks.

The blackness of George's moods is tellingly revealed when he acts out the role of a fanatic preacher who condemns Esther, a married woman, for her immoral behavior.

"Get right with Jesus, sister. He's here, watching you. He's standing at your shoulder this very minute, Sister Jack. . . . Do you hear him? He's speaking to me now, sister. . . . Tell her to sin no more, and to return again to lawful wedlock. Remove temptation from the path, my son. Arise and leave her."

He paused for a moment; he stared at her with a madman's burning love.

"The Lord is speaking to me, Sister Jack. He is telling me to leave you."

"You go to hell," she said.

Their differences grow wider and their words sharper, climaxing in Chapter 37, entitled "The Quarrel." Nevertheless, because of the depth of their love, moments of reconciliation are inevitable. George declares, "You are the woman that I love, and no matter where I go, or when I leave you, as I shall, down at the bottom of my soul I'll keep on loving you forever." Esther has assumed many roles—George's mistress, cook, mentor, patron, mother, and muse.[5] Accusations, fights, bitter leave-takings, and reconciliations exhaust the two and drive Esther to the brink of suicide. In the end, it is their respective work that saves them. Wolfe gives to Esther the more reflective and philosophical view of the affair: "The tears were flowing down her face, because she loved life dearly, and because all the triumphant music, the power, the glory, and the singing of proud love grew old and came to dust."

In addition to this central love story, Wolfe provides a secondary theme: the brashness of youth as revealed in George Webber's going to Europe determined to seek the mythical golden fleece; instead, Wolfe says, George returns almost penniless and like a shorn Jason. And before the affair with Esther actually begins, George dashes off a seventeen-page letter to express, he says, "his casual disinterest" in this woman. Hurt that Esther seems to be ignoring him, George thinks his letter will in part assuage his feelings. Although he shortens his diatribe to eleven pages before he mails it, it is still a ridiculous gesture of youthful excess. Wolfe, perhaps partially in self-chastisement, observes: "But of such is youth. And he was young." Other important ideas Wolfe presents are George's unrelenting desire for fame (Wolfe's image for fame is the beguiling Medusa) and his Faustian craving: "He would surfeit himself with everything that he could buy, with everything he could afford, with everything that he could see or hear or could remember, and still there was no end." Wolfe particularly extols Germany (in spite of the Oktoberfest fight in which he, and Monk, got their heads cracked)—its food, beer, people, art. Throughout all of George's adventures, Wolfe continues to deal with the mysterious force of time—that force which in the end controls the quest for fame and love and adventure.

As in *Look Homeward, Angel* and *Of Time*

and the River, satire appears frequently in *The Web and the Rock*. George ridicules theater-goers who try to show off, quoting one as saying of a new production, "Oh, no. The play is nothing, of course. But you really ought to see the sets." (And, of course, designing sets was Aline Bernstein's career.) He satirizes New York aesthetes who show up at parties, act absurdly and childishly, and form "a precious coterie." Prime examples are the arrogant and petulant poet Rosalind Bailey and the novelist Paul Van Vleek, who writes supposedly sophisticated books about tattooed duchesses, post-Impressionist moving-picture actresses, and black prize fighters who read Greek. The school where George teaches, The School of Utility Cultures, Inc., embodies the crass side of urban Americans, who seek to get ahead at any price. Through George Webber, Wolfe points out the difficulties he had in placing *Look Homeward, Angel*, a novel almost all publishers found too long and too autobiographical. The publishing house Boni and Liveright (which did reject Wolfe's novel) is called in the novel Rawng and Wright. Rawng, George charges, does not know how to read books, just how to publish them. His irritation with this publishing firm erupts in the doggerel couplets that end Chapter 23: "Poems are made by flame and song/But God knows who made Wright and Rawng."

Another satiric attack is leveled at Ernest Boyd, the agent and critic who gave Wolfe's first manuscript to his wife, Madeleine, without reading it. Boyd is called Seamus Malone, a man

George overhears at a party admitting that he *has* read a few pages of George's manuscript. Malone cries out,

"Not bad when compared to the backwoods bilge of Mr. Sinclair Lewis! Not bad when compared to the niggling nuances of that neurotic New Englander from Missouri, Mr. T. S. Eliot, who, after baffling an all-too-willing world for years by the production of such incomprehensible nonsense as *The Waste Land* and *The Love Song of J. Alfred Prufrock*, and gaining for himself a reputation for perfectly *enormous* erudition among the aesthetes of Kalamazoo by the production of verses in dog-Latin and rondels in bastard French that any convent school girl would be ashamed to acknowledge as her own, has now, my friends, turned prophet, priest, and political revolutionary."

In spite of this hyperbole, Malone nevertheless has a moment of calm in which in he offers hope at last to the young novelist: "Just for a moment the pale lips writhed tormented in his inky, blue-black beard, and then—oh, tormented web of race and man!—he got it out. He smiled at young Webber quite winningly and said: 'I liked your book. Good luck to you!'" Malone turns the manuscript over to the agent Lulu Scudder who "in turn did with it whatever it is that literary agents do, and in the end—yes, in the end—something came of it."

Wolfe makes these satiric attacks frequently in *The Web and the Rock*. He also makes effective use of literary and artistic allusions (especially to Brueghel's *The Land of Cockaigne*), catalogues, letters, and formal dialogue. Certainly the major symbols are clear enough: the web—growth, the creative principle—and the rock—the static quality that opposes growth (McElderry, p. 90). Furthermore, the first three books show Wolfe's strength in character portrayal and are remarkably free of the excesses that plague much of his writing. Even though the second part undoubtedly needs revision, it nevertheless conveys a memorable love story. Certainly *The Web and the Rock* must be considered in conjunction with *You Can't Go Home Again*, the continuation of George Webber's story. Viewed by itself, however, Wolfe's third novel is indeed unsatisfactory and provides strong evidence to many critics that if he was not a failed artist, he nonetheless had serious deficiencies as a writer. But it is also true that good writing is there in abundance; the novel does what good writing should always do—it evokes a response from readers and draws them back to the text again. One such passage occurs when George is on a channel steamer near Boulogne. In the early morning hours he explores the fabric of time and connects past and present. It is a long section, and almost any portion of it demonstrates that within this long novel, there are excellent parts:

Suddenly, just as they pass, a low, rich burst of laughter, tender and voluptuous, wells up out of the woman's throat, and at that moment, by the magic of time, a light burns on a moment of his weaving, a shutter is lifted in the dark, a lost moment lives again, and he hears at night, beneath the leafy rustle of mid-Summer trees, the feet of the lovers passing by along the street of a little town in America when he was nine years old, and the song they sang was "Love Me and the World is Mine."

Wolfe's fourth long book was *You Can't Go Home Again* (1940), a work of 742 pages that has drawn diverse reactions from critics. The late C. Hugh Holman considered it much less substantive a novel than *The Web and the Rock*,[6] and Richard Kennedy finds it choppier than the other titles, with the content thinly spread. However, Kennedy does conjecture that had Wolfe lived, *You Can't Go Home Again* "would have been longer and denser—perhaps his greatest book" (p. 410). On the other hand, Clyde C. Clements, Jr., argues that through certain symbolic patterns in this novel, Wolfe "rendered his lifetime experience and reflection into a meaningful art form."[7] And perhaps the strongest defense of the novel's composition comes from Herbert Muller, who finds it "clearly designed and solidly constructed" (p. 125).

Although Wolfe had given no final shape to this material before his death, Edward Aswell at that time cut, rearranged, and, more importantly, "tampered with Wolfe's style as he had not done before" (Kennedy, p. 403). Indeed, by juxtaposing portions of Wolfe's manuscript with Aswell's published version, Kennedy demonstrated in 1962 that "the hand of the editor intrudes more often in *You Can't Go Home Again* than readers have suspected. By this time, Aswell identified himself with Wolfe to the extent that he felt free to play author with the manuscript" (p. 405). Still, the critic must deal with the version Aswell published, since the likelihood of our ever seeing Wolfe's actual manuscript in print and in a comprehensible order is small.

You Can't Go Home Again remains an important book, in large measure because it most clearly reflects Wolfe's increased awareness and response to social problems. The pre-Depression real estate boom in Asheville, for example, was to Wolfe a paradigm of the corruption possible in human nature—from the citizens in Libya Hill who ruined natural surroundings and compromised their integrity in making paper fortunes to the Nazi persecutions that Wolfe witnessed in Germany in 1936. Wolfe did not become politically sophisticated, but he showed a breadth of understanding not present in his earlier books. In addition to well-drawn minor characters and effective satire, *You Can't Go Home Again* contains two of Wolfe's best and most objectively rendered pieces, "The Party at Jack's" and "I Have a Thing to Tell You."[8] Wolfe could be successful when his writing was lyrical and confessional; however, these traits often were excessive and sacrificed the control he could achieve through objective narration.

You Can't Go Home Again is divided into seven books with forty-eight titled chapters. Back from nine months in Europe, George Webber renews his relationship with Esther Jack. As George says, his head tells him to let the affair stay ended; his heart prompts him to see Esther once more. The second major event for him is the publication of his first novel. This episode introduces Wolfe's fictional version of Maxwell Perkins, Foxhall Edwards; Charles Scribner's Sons, James Rodney and Company; and *Scribner's Magazine, Rodney's Magazine,* and it constitutes a body of material that Perkins earlier told Wolfe might force him to resign from the firm if published. Much of this material Perkins had told Wolfe in confidence.

In many ways *You Can't Go Home Again* consists of a series of discoveries and losses.[9] George Webber's return to Libya Hill for Aunt Maw's funeral causes him to confront his mountain-bred kin, who will never understand his life as an artist. Further, Libya Hill has begun in earnest the mad financial boom that eventually produces forty suicides. Like many Wolfe characters, Webber learns that "you can't go home again." The appearance of *Home to Our Mountains* at last brings Webber fame, but it also brings the lion hunters who stalk the famous. Fame also brings bitter reactions from folks back home who are not pleased to recognize themselves and others in print. Webber must see that the longed-for fair Medusa is still capable of turning people to stone with a single glance. Webber's disillusionment with fame is further explored during his brief adventure with Lloyd McHarg (Sinclair Lewis) in England. Fame, he learns, does not guarantee common sense, good manners, or happiness. The renewal of love with Esther does not last, and he must again experience losing her. Finally, his realization that the Germany he loved is on the verge of political devastation shatters yet another happiness.

Holman's analysis demonstrates the two uncongenial themes in the novel, themes expressed in distinctly different stylistic modes: "rhetorical hope and dramatic despair" (p. 93). The latter is vividly portrayed by Nebraska Crane, who continues from *The Web and the Rock*. Crane is thirty-one when George meets up with him at Aunt Maw's funeral. Furloughed from his professional baseball team, Nebraska comes home with a pulled tendon in his right ankle and tells George his life is falling to pieces:

> "But I'm cracking up, Monkus. Guess I can't stan' the gaff much more."
> Nebraska was thirty-one, now, and George was incredulous.
> "That's an ole man in baseball, Monk. I went up when I was twenty-one. I been aroun' a long time."

Nebraska (speaking like Jack Keefe) does have the compensation of having been "in three World Serious,"[10] but, as with Jim Randolph in *The Web and the Rock*, his glory has been brief.

In Judge Rumford Bland, Wolfe symbolizes the corruption in Libya Hill. Although he is descended from a fine old family, Judge Bland is a blind, syphilitic man and a usurer whose only clients are ignorant blacks. As many critics have pointed out, Bland is a Tiresias figure, making lawyers, bankers, and real estate men nervous as his blind eyes see through their ten-

uous schemes. It is he who (by touch) discovers
the mayor's body in the City Hall washroom—
one of the forty suicides. His physical condition
is corrupt, he charges outrageous interest rates,
and he makes George Webber fear that he already knows that *Home to Our Mountains* is
an exposé of Libya Hill: "The blind man cackled
thinly to himself, enjoying with evil tenderness
his little cat's play with the young man: 'The
guilty fleeth where no man pursueth. Is that it,
son?'" The oxymoron "evil tenderness" and
the Scripture-quoting line reflect Bland's
twisted nature as well as the blighted nature of
the town. The citizens have demolished fine old
structures and leveled green hills to make way
for paved parking lots and the Libya-Ritz. Even
the local newspaper reporter distorts the truth
to suit himself. During an interview, his questions bring only hesitant and broken answers
from George, but his published article is an altogether different account. The reporter asks
George how Libya Hill compares to other places
he visited. George replies, "Why—Why—er—
why *good!* . . . I mean *fine!* That is—." The
news story lead, however, is "Local Paradise
Compares Favorably," and the article has the
reporter's lies, not George's words: "'It shall be
part of my purpose from now on,' the earnest
young author added, 'to do everything in my
power to further this great cause, and to urge
all my writing and artistic friends to settle
here—to make Libya Hill the place it ought to
be—The Athens of America.'"[11]

A more bitter example of dramatic despair
is Wolfe's scathing satire of the Federal Weight,

Scales, and Computing Company. Its jargon repeats America's success slogans: "The Company," "Creative Salesmanship," "Creating the Market," "The Sales Organization." When the president addresses his sales force at the national convention, he sweeps his arm over a huge map of the United States and says, "There's your market! Go out and sell them!" The narrative voice roundly satirizes such business practices:

What could be simpler and more beautiful than this? What could more eloquently indicate that mighty sweep of the imagination which has been celebrated in the annals of modern business under the name of "vision"? The words had the spacious scope and austere directness that have characterized the utterances of great leaders in every epoch of man's history. It is Napoleon speaking to his troops in Egypt: "Soldiers, from the summit of yonder pyramids, forty centuries look down upon you." It is Captain Perry: "We have met the enemy, and they are ours." It is Dewey at Manila Bay: "You may fire when ready, Gridley." It is Grant before Spottsylvania Court House: "I propose to fight it out on this line, if it takes all summer."

This commercial mania reduces George's friend Randy Shepperton to a nervous wreck. When Randy is fired, he is sure he will be all right—a salesman simply changes products and finds another job. But no job is to be had, Randy's savings are exhausted, and he has no recourse but to go on relief. Through the plight of Randy Shepperton Wolfe debunks the American dream of advertising and big business. Prosperity, rugged individualism, and the American way have become nothing but catch phrases. Through Libya Hills' collective collapse and that of Randy Shepperton, Wolfe shows the effects of the Depression at home. When he moved the scene to Manhattan, Brooklyn, and London, he was equally graphic in portraying poverty, hunger, and hopelessness.

The reality of social and economic class differences dominates Book III, which Wolfe entitled "The World That Jack Built." Wolfe separately presents Mr. and Mrs. Jack as they rise to meet the day. At 7:28 A.M. Mr. Jack wakes and in his ninth floor Park Avenue apartment begins his daily ritual amidst every imaginable luxury. Although fine things also surround Mrs. Jack, Wolfe emphasizes her creative talent and her bright appeal: "When she came into a room she filled it with her loveliness and gave to everything about her the color of morning life and innocence." And he draws a sharp contrast between Esther—bright, hard-working, creative—and her maid Nora, who is surly, indolent, and constantly drinking. Even Nora knows that wealth has not spoiled Mrs. Jack: "There was no task in all the household range of duties, whether of serving, mending, cooking, cleaning, or repairing which her mistress could not do far better and with more dispatch than she." Wolfe is not presenting the idle rich; both Mr. and Mrs. Jack have important and productive careers. The reality of the 1929 stock market crash and the ruined fortunes that followed are foreshadowed here in two episodes. As Mr. Jack with great contentment surveys the furnishings of his bedroom, he sees a four-poster bed of the Revolutionary period, an antique chest of drawers, a gate-legged table, two fine old Windsor chairs, several charming French prints on the walls, and thick and heavy carpet, all tastefully arranged. As he looks around him, a trembling is felt from the underground train lines far below the building. The sound and vibrations of the train bring to Mr. Jack "an old unquiet feeling to which he could not give a name." The most substantial luxury is threatened; the trembling from beneath the earth heralds the collapse that is nearly at hand.

The second episode is the party that the Jacks host. Here George Webber feels awkward and left out since in this setting his mistress now assumes her other roles—mistress of a Park Avenue dwelling and hostess to the wealthy and famous. Wolfe brings a climax to the entertainment with the appearance of Piggy Logan and his circus, the mechanical dolls and animals of Alexander Calder that were, as Wolfe says of Piggy Logan, "the rage." (The Bernsteins did in fact have Alexander Calder and his circus as the entertainment at a party.) The presentation is distasteful in every way. Logan temporarily destroys the Jacks' comfortable and charming living room to make room for his performance. A group of his young followers rudely crash the party to watch the show, whose climax is a grotesque sword-swallowing scene. As Logan has difficulty thrusting the sword down the doll's mouth, he persists until "the bulging doll was torn open and some of her stuffing began to ooze out." Disgusted, Mr. Jack an-

nounces that he is going to his room and departs
with the hope that the furniture will be left after
this display. Here Wolfe harshly satirizes New
York society of 1929. The narrative voice says,

to a future world—inhabited, no doubt, by a less
acute and understanding race of men—all this may
seem a trifle strange. If so, that will be because the
world of the future will have forgotten what it was
like to live in 1929. . . . Life had recently become
too short for many things that people had once found
time for. Life was simply too short for the perusal
of any book longer than two hundred pages. As for
War and Peace—[12] no doubt all "they" said of it was
true—but as for oneself—well, one had tried, and
really it was quite too—too—oh, well, life simply
was too short. So life that year was far too short to
be bothered by Tolstoy, Whitman, Dreiser, or Dean
Swift. But life was not too short that year to be pas-
sionately concerned with Mr. Piggy Logan and his
circus of wire dolls.

The party comes to a sudden end when the
cry "Fire!" is heard. Wolfe shows the escape
from the darkened, luxurious, and now vulnerable building to the sidewalk outside. All
classes mix—servants beside mistresses and famous guests. For the wealthy inhabitants of the
building tragedy is averted, since the fire is con-
fined to the basement; the subways are flooded,
not their elegant rooms. Just as the doorman has
protected the genteel tenants from panhandlers
at the building's entrance, so are they now shel-
tered from the knowledge that two employees
died in the fire. (Wolfe uses this same situation
in the Daisy Purvis section. A charwoman in

London, Daisy keeps up Webber's rooms, cooks his meals, and repeatedly tells him that the royalty are being taxed out of their estates. She and thousands like her, Daisy declares, can survive hard times and suffering, but the British royalty must be shielded from such distress: "'Ah-h yes,' she answered quietly, in a tone that was soft and gentle, as if she were speaking of the welfare of a group of helpless children, 'but then, we're used to it, *aren't* we? And they, poor things, they're not.'")

The snug nests of the Park Avenue residents are not destroyed by fire, and they return to their Windsor chairs and four-poster beds. But the experience shows George Webber that Esther's world of wealth and fashion is one into which he does not fit, and at the end of this long evening, George "got up and with a sick and tired heart he went away." Love, as this chapter title declares, is not enough. Implicit too is the impending Wall Street crash, which will again force Park Avenue residents from their snug nests. This time, however, they will not be protected, and they will not return to their routines unscathed.

Dramatic despair is central in Book VI when George Webber, now a famous author, arrives in Germany. It is 1936, and he is greeted and lionized by the public. Furthermore, he finds a new love in Else von Kohler. But from his friend Franz Heileg, Webber learns of the sad changes overcoming Germany. In the streets he hears the sounds of marching steps, and in the Belgium-bound train he and others try unsuccessfully to help a nervous Jewish lawyer cross

the border with his money. The few coins that
Webber had pocketed for the man seem tokens
of betrayal, as he watches the Nazis take the
Jew from the compartment and end his hopes
of freedom and safety. The incident is, as the
other passengers remark, "a sad end to our journey"; a German woman, still voicing love of
country, nonetheless adds quietly, "We are so
happy to be—*out!*" The ending of this section,
"I Have a Thing to Tell You," is Wolfe's final
tribute to Germany: "With all the measure of
your truth, your glory, beauty, magic, and your
ruin; and dark Helen in our blood, great queen
and mistress, sorceress—dark land, dark land,
old ancient earth I love—farewell!"

The extent of despair, of disillusionment
and loss, is great; but balance is indeed main-
tained, especially in Chapter 31, "The Promise
of America." Even though Wolfe describes here
George Webber's loneliness and difficulties
with fame, he sets forth also the terrain of
America from the Rocky Mountains to Chica-
go's south side, from all the cities of California
to the clay-baked Southern Piedmont. Although
in these places there is much poverty and difficulty, there remains hope for the good life:
"So, then, to every man his chance—to every
man, regardless of his birth, his shining, golden
opportunity—to every man the right to live, to
work, to be himself, and to become whatever
thing his manhood and his vision can combine
to make him—this, seeker, is the promise of
America."

Wolfe's use of "man" and "manhood" here
seems more a conscious than a random choice

of words. Generally in his fiction, Wolfe associates strength of spirit and success in work with male characters. Seldom does a woman achieve success. (If one considers Eliza Gant's boarding house and real estate ventures financial successes, the point must be made that they come at the expense of family happiness and cohesiveness. Esther Jack is indeed a success in her profession and a spiritual support for George; yet in the end she fails in the complicated relationships that love demands.) Wolfe seldom considers the role and potential of women; it is "every man" who will fulfill the promises, and it is "every man" who is "the promise of America." Certainly the passage is one of many that illustrate Wolfe's "rhetorical hope," but in a way of which he himself was probably conscious, the passage is, in ignoring women, one of "dramatic despair."

You Can't Go Home Again is an early portrayal in American literature of the artist in America. In a country given to getting and spending, the claims of art are difficult, if not impossible, for families like the Gants and Webbers and Joyners to understand. And artists like Eugene Gant and George Webber must leave those families for more hospitable people. As Howells and Twain moved east, as James moved to London, and as the generation of the twenties went to Paris, so Wolfe's artist must also leave home. Furthermore, because *You Can't Go Home Again* is not tainted with propaganda, it remains a novel that is a "comprehensive, searching report of the depression era" (Muller, p. 137). The banks in Libya Hill fail,

Wall Street crashes, people in hamlets and in cities commit suicide,[13] and the Daisy Purvises of this world know that poverty is a fact of life: "The idea that anything could or should be done about the sufferings of the poor never enters her head."

The thirty-seven-page letter from George Webber to Foxhall Edwards does not conclude the novel realistically or artistically. Filled with self-indulgent sentiments, needless repetitions, and self-analysis, the passage nevertheless contains Wolfe's most positive statement about America. Such a passage is still stirring and hopeful to read—"rhetorical hope" at its best— and it represents an optimism that was part of Wolfe's being:

I think the true discovery of America is before us. I think the true fulfillment of our spirit, of our people, of our mighty and immortal land, is yet to come. I think the true discovery of our own democracy is still before us. And I think that all these things are certain as the morning, as inevitable as noon. I think I speak for most men living when I say that our America is Here, is Now, and beckons on before us, and this glorious assurance is not only our living hope, but our dream to be accomplished.

4

From Death to Morning,
The Hills Beyond, and the
Short Novels
*
Failure, Success?

Aₗₜₕₒᵤ𝓰ₕ Wolfe's long-range goal was to complete the series of novels (in reality, one long novel) he had announced in the preface to *Of Time and the River*, his earliest ambition had been to write drama, a genre for which he had little affinity. As his career developed, various pressures and opportunities led him to write short stories and short novels; these works display considerable skill. Although they are read less frequently than *Look Homeward, Angel* or *Of Time and the River*, these shorter works constitute a significant part of Wolfe's life and work.

Wolfe's flirtation with drama began in his Chapel Hill days with his studies under Frederick Koch and his student efforts at acting and playwriting. The most notable of these modest achievements was *The Return of Buck Gavin*, a play in which Wolfe also acted and that Koch included in the second edition of *Carolina Folk Plays* (1924). Another undergraduate effort, *Concerning Honest Bob*, a slight but amusing view of campus politics, was given a successful performance in 1980 at St. Mary's College. (Richard Walser discusses all of Wolfe's undergraduate efforts at drama in *Thomas Wolfe Undergraduate*.[1]) Wolfe's interest in drama was the reason he went to Harvard in 1920 to enroll in George Pierce Baker's 47 Workshop, and a letter to Koch shows Wolfe's early enthusiasm: "I'm reading voraciously in the drama, stocking up with materials the same as a carpenter carries a mouthful of nails: I am studying plays, past and present, and the technique of these plays, emphasis, suspense, clearness, plot, proportion, and all the rest, and I've come to realize that this doctrine of divine inspiration is as damnable as that of the divine right of kings."[2]

Among Wolfe's belongings now in the Thomas Wolfe Collection at the University of North Carolina is a small calendar and engagement book for the 1921–1922 academic year. He made only a few entries, but two successive ones concern his one-act play *The Mountains*. On Friday, October 21, 1921, he recorded its first performance at Radcliffe's Agassiz Theater and commented, "acting discouraging." The second performance took place the next evening, and Wolfe was encouraged enough to write, "Cast a little better. Play must be condensed."[3] The last comment was advice Wolfe needed for almost everything he ever wrote.

Wolfe's major effort in Baker's class began as a play called "Niggertown," which was retitled *Welcome to Our City*. A sharp and often overdone criticism of urban and industrial society, the play has an excessively large cast as well as unwieldly stage directions and sets. When the 47 Workshop produced the play, the response was mixed. In the audience was an Asheville native who exclaimed with consternation that she recognized almost every character. This 1923 production was not an unqualified success for Wolfe.

As many critics have pointed out, Wolfe's other major dramatic effort, *Mannerhouse*, does not mark any progress over *Welcome to Our City*. Like the earlier play, *Mannerhouse* criticizes urban and industrial society; however, it does have an interesting history. The plot came from an episode W. O. had related to Wolfe and that Wolfe pondered during the years he attended Baker's class. A play did not result until 1925.[4] (Among the various titles he considered were "The Heirs," "The Wasters," and "The House.") The manuscript was stolen during Wolfe's first trip to Europe when a lazy concierge left one of Wolfe's three heavy suitcases in the lobby. The loss at first seemed catastrophic, but Wolfe set to work rewriting and settled on the title *Mannerhouse*. As Andrew Turnbull (p. 89) notes, Wolfe considered this new version the best work he had done. However, in spite of some encouragement, *Manner-house*, like *Welcome to Our City*, was not accepted by New York theater groups. Although Helen Arthur and Agnes Morgan realized that the play was hopeless as drama, they also recognized Wolfe's writing talent, and their Neighborhood Playhouse colleague, Aline Bernstein (who had not yet met Wolfe), took the manuscript to Europe for Alice Lewisohn to read. Lewisohn's rejection, however, was not the end of the story. On July 1, 1949, Edward Aswell (executor of Wolfe's estate after Max Perkins's death) reported to Mabel Wolfe Wheaton that he had signed an agreement with New Stage, Inc., for a New York production of the play. Plans fell through and no New York performance was given, although in 1953 and in 1956 successful performances were staged in Germany (Rice, p. 33).

Mannerhouse consists of a prologue and three acts that stretch in time from the late colonial period until post-Reconstruction. The Ramsey family lives in a house built by slaves (the leader of the slaves had been a king and was subdued in slavery only by violence). The common Southern themes of family, honor, and manners are present, although the rather liberal son Eugene Ramsey is a temporary disruption of the tradition. A more permanent disruption, of course, is the Civil War. In the character named Porter, Wolfe creates a Snopesian figure who starts from nothing, slinks obsequiously about, enters the lumber business, and ends up owning the Ramsey house and property. All of Porter's actions lack decorum. He takes his son out of the army to work the fields at home; he hates "niggers" and calls them black bastards. He touches objects in the Ramsey house with filthy and covetous fingers, and when the property must at last be given up to him, he insists that General Ramsey put "h't on paper—to do hit legal." Porter, as the General says, possesses all of the ingredients for worldly success and none of those for success as a gentleman. Furthermore, Wolfe gives him a repulsive appearance: "his dress is common and his body meager; and . . . his face is small, narrow, mean and pinched." The silver coins he jingles in his pockets symbolize his crassness. At the end of Act III, Eugene, now a mill worker, comes back to what had been his home and is taken for a tramp by Porter's carpenters. In a melodramatic ending, Eugene, Samsonlike, places gaunt arms around the porch columns, calling out his failure to the old family slave Tod. Then, in a terrible crash, he brings the house down on his past.

The play is weak. It lacks thematic focus, stage directions often are far too detailed, and too many special effects are called for. In addition, there are stilted dialogue, wooden female characters, a central character who makes endless references to Shakespeare, stereotypic black–white relationships, and melodramatic attitudes about "the war." *Mannerhouse* is the play that Eugene Gant reads to Joel Pierce and his sister Rosalind in *Of Time and the River*. In the novel, the play's subject is described as the "decline and ultimate extinction of a proud old family of the Southern aristocracy in years after the Civil War," and the narrative voice admits it "was written in a somewhat mixed mood of romantic sentiment, Byronic irony, and sardonic realism." By the time he wrote these words, Wolfe probably saw clearly the thinness of his dramatic effort. One can easily see why New York theatrical groups turned the play down in 1925 and 1926.

When Alice Lewisohn offered Wolfe no encouragement from the Neighborhood Playhouse and all his other plans for writing and producing drama seemed to fail, *Mannerhouse* "was mysteriously dropped, and Wolfe started work on *Look Homeward, Angel* (Rice, p. 32). Maxwell Perkins's recollection about Wolfe and drama was revealing: Perkins said that Wolfe regarded actors with "complete contempt. He often talked of the stage with scorn, and I used to think it was partly because of the artificiality of the whole thing, the meanness of spending one's life pretending to be somebody you're not."[5] Wolfe's attempts at drama brought him much criticism and disappointment, and although drama gave him a reason for writing, the genre was altogether inappropriate for his effusive style. The years spent on drama added little to Wolfe's career; they did, however, lead him to think of himself as a writer.

Although Wolfe published many short stories, he admitted that he did not know what magazines wanted and declared he would "like nothing better than to write something that was both very good and very popular: I should be enchanted if the editors of *Cosmopolitan* began to wave large fat checks under my nose, but I know of no ways of going about this deliberately and I am sure I'd fail miserably if I tried" (*Letters*, p. 325). Most often his short stories were segments of the larger manuscript he was always working on at the time, and he felt uncertain about excising a portion and shaping it as a short story. Once when he sent Elizabeth Nowell approximately seven typed pages out of a manuscript (a piece about two boys going to the circus) he wrote, "The thing ["Circus at Dawn"] needs an introduction which I will try to write today, but otherwise it is complete enough, although, again, I am afraid it is not what most people consider a story" (*Letters*, p. 402). ("Circus at Dawn" was published in *Modern Monthly* in 1935; it was also included in *From Death to Morning*.) Wolfe generally left such decisions and selections up to Nowell.

All fourteen stories that *From Death to Morning* (1935) comprises appeared in magazines or academic journals between July 1932, when "The Web of Earth" was published, and October 1935, when "The Bums at Sunset" appeared. Seven of these stories were published by *Scribner's Magazine*, two by *Modern Monthly*, and one each by *The New Yorker*, *Vanity Fair*, *Cosmopolitan*, *Harper's Bazaar*, and the *Virginia Quarterly Review*—a wide variety of publications. Letters in 1933 indicate that Wolfe was hard pressed for money; selling stories was therefore essential. He was down to $7, he said, when the sale of "No Door" to *Scribner's Magazine* brought him $200. Although he welcomed this sum, Wolfe wrote George Wallace (a former member of Professor Baker's 47 Workshop at Harvard) that he was considering taking his stories to another agent, one who had indicated he could get higher prices than *Scribner's Magazine*, Wolfe's most frequent publisher, offered. Obviously Wolfe would indeed welcome "large fat checks" from *Cosmopolitan*. These stories earned him funds first as single sales and then in the collected volume *From Death to Morning*. This volume appeared eight months after *Of Time and the River* was published, making 1935 an important year of publication for Wolfe.

Wolfe attributed the unenthusiastic reviews of *From Death to Morning* to the criticism that continued to be made about *Of Time and the River*: excessive length. The favorable reviews stressed the lyrical prose, humor, realism, and engaging characters. Nevertheless, this neglected volume generally has been underrated, with just a few stories receiving serious attention; indeed, Richard Kennedy thinks that *From Death to Morning* is a book that discourages a second reading. While critics wisely avoid extravagant claims for this collection, they need not shy away from confidently praising Wolfe's variety of narrative forms, his range of subject matter, the large number of effectively drawn characters, the careful attention to place, and the emotional power. Indeed, emotional power is the significant feature, one that Wolfe conveys best through a pervasive feeling of loneliness in characters and through some extraordinarily violent scenes.

Narrative forms include the episodic, epistolary, stream-of-consciousness, as well as slice-of-life, the form that describes "Only the Dead Know Brooklyn" and "The Bums at Sunset." Each of these stories concerns a problem, for which no solution is reached. Like most of the stories in this collection, these two implicitly explore the theme of loneliness that is prevalent even in "The Web of Earth," a piece of writing whose main character, Wolfe says, "is grander, richer and more tremendous" than Joyce's Molly Bloom at the end of *Ulysses* (*Letters*, p. 339). In both "Only the Dead Know Brooklyn" and "The Bums at Sunset," the characters are flat, distinguished only by age and basic reactions. The bums are a chance collection of lonely men exiled for unknown reasons from families and productive work. Both stories center on the arrival of a stranger. In "The Bums at Sunset," the appearance of the young, uninitiated bum threatens those who know the ropes and are suspicious of his lack of experience. "What is dis anyway?" one of them sneers, "a - - - - noic'ry [nursery], or sump'n." In "Only the Dead Know Brooklyn," the big guy who presumes to learn all of Brooklyn by asking directions and studying his map baffles the narrator, who declares, "Dere's no guy livin' dat knows Brooklyn t'roo and t'roo."[6] While the voice of the Brooklyn native narrates this story, an omniscient voice tells the story of "The Bums at Sunset," and his diction contrasts with the bums' ungrammatical speech and limited vocabulary in its use of figurative language; for example, the fading light of sunset looks, he says, "like a delicate and ancient bronze." And in picturing these nondescript men, the narrator emphasizes that their inescapable loneliness tells "a legend of pounding wheel and thrumming rod, of bloody brawl and brutal shambles, of the savage wilderness, the wild, cruel and lonely distances of America."

"Gulliver," a brief character study of an excessively tall man, relates the discomfort of someone who never fits into chairs, beds, or Pullman car berths—of a giant in a world of normal-sized people. Furthermore, the central character is subjected to the same insults wherever he goes: "Hey-y, Mis-teh! . . . Is it rainin' up deh?" His physical size dominates the story and causes the pain and incommunicable loneliness that mark his life. In "The Far and the Near," a very short piece originally entitled "The Cottage by the Tracks," Wolfe tells a sentimental story about a railroad engineer who finally discovers the reality of what he had thought to be an idyllic scene: a mother and a daughter who live in a country cottage near the tracks. For twenty years the engineer has waved to them as his train roared past, and now that he has retired, he comes to greet them in person. From the moment the older woman opens the door, he knows he should not have come. The idyllic scene he saw for years now fades before her suspicious attitude, her harsh voice, and her unsmiling face. The engineer is left disappointed and lonely, since the reality of the unfriendly cottage inhabitants precludes his hopes of friendship with them and indeed ruins his memory. If the engineer has any other life to go to, we are not told of it.

The subjects of loneliness and death coalesce in the story of the dying man in "Dark in the Forest, Strange as Time." Because he is ill, the man must go away alone for the winter to warmer climate; his wife promises that she will join him in the spring. Other people board the train, many of them talking and laughing as they leave. The dying man's wife settles him in the compartment, turns, and quickly leaves to join her young, robust lover who waits on the platform. This desertion is repeated in a lesser way with the American youth assigned to this same compartment. His good health and youth contrast sharply with the dying man's condition. And when the youth leaves the compartment for the conviviality of the dining car, the older man dies. He never fulfills his modest desire of knowing well just "vun field, vun hill, vun riffer."

As it appears in *From Death to Morning*, "No Door"[7] is only the first segment of a much longer work of the same title, a short novel Max Perkins considered bringing out in a limited edition. He did not do so, however. In the original version, this first segment is subtitled "October 1931." Structurally, the brief version in *From Death to Morning* fails to develop a unified plot. The story begins in the luxurious apartment of the host, a rich man who has taken the requisite trip to Europe, collected a suitably impressive collection of sculpture and rare books, and lives among furnishings that are of "quiet but distinguished taste." His young mistress is at his side when his guest (a writer) relates painful glimpses of Brooklyn's low life. The host appears to listen, but he responds incon-

gruously—"grand," "marvelous," "swell"—
even though the young man tells of men who
live in alleyways, beat their wives, and consider
murder and robbery honest toil. In some detail
the guest relates an episode about the loud demands of a lonely prostitute for her $3 payment.
Her client refuses to pay her until, as he puts
it, she will "staht actin' like a lady." Oblivious
to the irony, the host continues to murmur
"grand," and he envies the young man the rich
experience of living among such people.

In the final pages Wolfe abandons the host,
his mistress, the tinkling cocktail glasses, and
the penthouse balcony to recount the haunting
story of a priest's death. One of Wolfe's finest
vignettes, this episode stays in the narrator's
mind "like the haunting refrain of some old
song—as it was heard and lost in Brooklyn." At
evening, a man and a woman appear in their
respective apartment windows to talk, their
voices issuing banalities such as "Wat's t' noos
sinct I been gone?" Although Father Grogan has
died while this speaker was away, the priest's
death is little more than a piece of news to be
reported by one nameless character to another.
It is not a grief to be shared, as one can see by
the response to the news: "Gee, dat's too bad
. . . I musta been away. Oddehwise I woulda
hoid." Although the narrator is fully aware of
the tragic implications of the priest's death, he
makes no overt judgments about the insensitive
speakers. The scene ends with a simple line: "A
window closed, and there was silence." The casual announcement of Father Grogan's death and
the equally casual reaction lead the narrator to

consider time, in whose relentless power fame is lost, names are forgotten, and energy is wasted. Indeed, Father Grogan and all mankind die in darkness; they are remembered only superficially, if at all.

Related as it is to loneliness and violence, the theme of human dejection is present throughout these stories. The host may be wealthy, but he is a man who has never really lived. Indeed, Wolfe says this man measures time not by actual deeds but "in dimensions of fathomless and immovable sensations." His young guest lives in a run-down section of Brooklyn, an environment in stark contrast to his host's penthouse. When the young man describes the abject conditions of his neighborhood, the host considers such tales colorful and alive, unlike his own rich but dead world. The diverse reactions of these two men cannot be reconciled. The unrelieved loneliness, the failure of communication, and the narrator's search for certitude and meaning are problems introduced but left unresolved. Solutions are hinted at through brief passages whose imagery expresses a momentary harmony—"all of the colors of the sun and harbor, flashing, blazing, shifting in swarming motes, in an iridescent web of light and color for an instant on the blazing side of a proud white ship." The color flashes and then is gone, however; what remains for the narrator is unspeakable loneliness.

Like "Only the Dead Know Brooklyn" and "Dark in the Forest, Strange as Time," this short version of "No Door" is a poignant examination of people who do not know how to express their deepest feelings, of people who do not or cannot share the burden or happiness of another, of people who are overwhelmed by loneliness.

In June 1935, *Modern Monthly* published Wolfe's story "The Face of War." Much of the plot stems from the summer of 1918, when Wolfe worked in the Norfolk shipyards. Like "Death the Proud Brother" (the story that follows "The Face of War" in *From Death to Morning*) this story focuses on four separate episodes, uses shocking violence, and emphasizes loneliness. In the first episode, Wolfe objectively relates the senseless beating of a black construction worker at Langley Field by the slouchy, shambling figure of a Southern white man who is egged on by his worthless office clerk. Wolfe's imagery suggests the bestial nature of these characters. The white boss wields a club "in his meaty hand," and his abnormal voice is described "as high thick throat-scream of blood-lust and murder." His office clerk creeps about "with rat's teeth bared" and "the coward's lust to kill." The clerk keeps a safe distance from the black man and urges his boss "to shoot the bastard if he tries to hit you." After the beating, the black man staggers about with a broken nose, buckling knees, and a ripped skull. He had seen the enemy coming and had half crouched, "ape-like" with arms like "great paws." His "white eyeballs" were now fixed, and he was ready to leap or run. The victim never utters a word and finally is left unconscious before his enemies. The "paunch-gut man" and his "white rat-face" clerk behind him beat the black man because the boss will be damned "if a God-damn Nigger can talk back to a white man." This episode is particularly important since Wolfe does not include many black characters or often present racial issues and confrontations in his fiction. While he by no means attacks the subject with Faulkner's eye for its complexity, Wolfe was neither callous nor oblivious to the injustices that befell blacks.

Violence also erupts in the second episode of "The Face of War" when three young, friendly, blue-eyed, slow-talking Southern men appear. Having finished their construction job for the day, they are stopped abruptly by a foul-mouthed armed guard who accuses them of mischief. He pulls his gun, snarls, and stares at them with "eyes a-glitter, narrow as a snake." The guard's senseless verbal attack bewilders them. His crude words contrast sharply with the calm passage that had earlier described the boys as they walked near the water's edge, talking of home, college, and plans for the weekend.

Throughout the story the August sun beats mercilessly, and in the third episode it shines on the raw pine brothel set up hastily in war-time. Recruited from northern and midwestern cities, the prostitutes are neither alluring nor beautiful, and their aggressive behavior covers any display of tenderness. The men are name-less except for one called Georgia. Dressed in khaki uniforms, they stand in line, impatiently calling to the occupants of the tiny cubicles to "come on out an' give some of duh rest of us a

chanct, f'r Chris' sake!" The prostitutes are ra-
pacious, weary-eyed, and hard-visaged. Their
obscene language contrasts ironically with another side of them, which Wolfe describes as a
"fearful, almost timid desire to find friendship,
gentleness, and even love among the rabble-rout
of lost and ruined men to whom they minister."
Georgia recognizes a prostitute named Margaret
as a girl from home. As if they had met under
proper social circumstances, she says, "How are
all the folks down home? . . . Tell'em that I sent
my love." She prods the youth to promise that
he will "ask for Margaret" next time, and then
she is gone, "engulfed into the great vortex of
the war." With this unseemly collection of men
and women, Wolfe symbolizes the chaotic conditions of wartime, when virtue and life are easily destroyed.

The fourth episode concerns a paternalistic
army lieutenant who curses at but also protects
his black charges. The loading dock is suffo-
catingly hot as food and munitions of all sorts
are put on the war-bound ship. Described by the
lieutenant as "poor dumb suffering second cousins of an owl," the black troops are nearly left
behind, since they have not been cleared of venereal disease. Because the lieutenant inter-
venes at the last minute, they are once again
checked and this time declared clean by the
ship's doctor and allowed to board. Clamoring
their gratitude to the white man, they rush forward, bound for war and probable death.

"The Face of War" is filled with ironic jux-
tapositions. The tranquility of civilian life gives
way to the harsh demands of wartime. Ships

carry both food and weapons; the companion-
ship of the troops contrasts with their eagerness
to kill the enemy; and the raw, sensual, make-
shift brothel is the opposite of the old life Margaret and Georgia knew back home in Hope-
well. At the end of the story, the ship is loaded,
shouting is replaced by silence, and the oppres-
sive heat yields to "the breath of coolness."
Death may await the ship's occupants, but for
this night they remain in "the oncoming, un-
dulant stride of all-enfolding and deep-breasted
night."

One of the longest stories in *From Death
to Morning*, "Death the Proud Brother," tells of
four deaths in New York City that the narrator
witnesses. The first three are violent and occur
in different locations at different times of the
year. In a swift and horrifying accident, an Italian street vendor is killed by a truck on a spring
day. For five pages, Wolfe presents details that
characterize the nameless victim. His small
pots and pans now are rubble, and his blood
stains the sidewalk that a shop owner rushes
out to clean. Business resumes and the street
vendor drops from the memory of those who
saw him daily. Related in six pages, the second
death occurs in a new downtown building on
an icy night in February when a drunken bum
falls into a pile of iron beams and smashes his
head. Wolfe then devotes twelve pages to the
third death, that of a rivet catcher who misses
the fiery steel tossed to his bucket and plunges
to his death. The time is a May morning, ironically bright and sparkling. In contrast to the
violence of these three is the fourth death, that

of a nondescript man sitting on a subway bench; he collapses almost imperceptibly. Wolfe takes twenty-six pages to relate this final episode, which occurs at 1:00 A.M. in the Times Square station.

Each death involves the reactions of strangers. City people, the narrator thinks, accept death, "its violence, bloody mutilation, and horror calmly as one of the natural consequences of daily life." For example, a wealthy lady praises her chauffeur when he extricates her car quickly from the traffic snarl following the construction worker's death. To many onlookers, this dead man is a mere statistic: "Say—dat makes duh fourt' one on dat building—did yuh know dat?" Youthful onlookers are singularly unsympathetic, existing as testimony to "a new and desolate race of youth upon the earth that men had never known before—a race hard, fruitless, and unwholesome." They are simply curious and momentarily diverted; to them grief is "out of date and falsely sentimental." Older witnesses are equally insensitive and are interested only in repeating the news: "Sure! I seen it! I seen it! Dat's what I'm tellin' yuh!" Policemen, interns, and priests perform their respective functions because they must. In the end, the police tell the crowds, "Yuh gotta move. It's all oveh," more concerned with restoring the flow of traffic than with the fact of death. Such a sweeping judgment of city dwellers makes Wolfe's criticism somewhat stereotyped; nevertheless, although he was a city dweller all of his adult life, he did remain somewhat apart from the city and somewhat suspicious of its natives.

Regardless of their backgrounds, witnesses to violent, bloody, fatal accidents press forward to stare; however, people confronted with the quiet death of the man in the subway stand back timidly. "Stunned, awed, bewildered, and frightened," they see that a man's death can come so quietly that it is difficult to perceive. In a way, this death is the most frightening because it reminds us that we face death alone. The youthful narrator, moved by these tragedies, quotes the line from a Thomas Nashe poem on the plague year, "Brightness falls from the air." Nevertheless, the narrator's own youth and vigor make him hopeful about the future: "I knew I should see light once more and know new coasts and come into strange harbors, and see again, as I had once, new lands and morning." Such bursts of lyricism are poignantly juxtaposed to the realistic details of death and dying.

Stylistically, much of "Death the Proud Brother" is starkly realistic. For instance, when the callous young couple pass the corpse of the bum, they look at him and remark that perhaps he might join their late night excursion: "Who *else* can we get?" they remark. Further, as the policemen remove the dead man from the subway station, they grumble when the lifeless arms tumble off the stretcher, and they finally secure them with the man's own necktie. Once they reach the street, a taxi driver "lifted his cap obsequiously to the dead man. 'Taxi, sir!

Taxi!'" The policemen laugh and swear. Concrete details enhance the powerful realism in many parts of the story. For example, we are told that the Italian vendor's cart held such things as cheap candies, a greasy-looking orange-juice bottle, cheap knives, and a small oil stove. Although similes, metaphors, apostrophes, hyperbole, and catalogues are used effectively in this story, the image of the clicking turnstiles in the subway emitting their dull wooden notes perhaps makes the most profound impression. Through those turnstiles scurry passengers who rush to meet their schedules, and their routine leaves little time even to observe that a man has died. The dead man in the subway will probably go to a pauper's grave, mourned and remembered by none. All four of these victims led commonplace lives, but each is given "for an instant the immortal dignities of death, proud death, even when it rested on the poorest cipher in the street."

By far the most significant selection in *From Death to Morning* is the long story (or novella) "The Web of Earth." This piece, a complicated monologue delivered by Eliza Gant to her son during a visit to his Brooklyn Heights apartment, consists of tales linked weblike by the filament of association. A word or a sound in the tale she is telling sends Eliza to another story, but no matter how far the new directions takes her, she retraces her steps, finishing each tale in turn. She begins with her earliest recollections at age two and continues with events from childhood, marriage, motherhood, and old age. Her memories are almost all sad and pain-

ful, but her spirit is resilient. The first tale is of
men she saw returning from the Civil War shoe-
less, hungry, aged; their joy in reunion is un-
dercut by their lament for the dead. Her other
childhood memories are of vicious tricks played
by brothers, sisters, and cousins on each other;
she does not relate any pleasant childhood adventures.

Recollections of W. O.'s imprudent behavior color her memories about married life. Once
when Eliza was pregnant and W. O. had begun
a drinking spree, she walked into Ambrose Radiker's saloon and demanded that he sell W. O.
no more liquor. It was a request Radiker would
gladly have granted if he could, since W. O.
often attacked the saloon's light-skinned black
worker. W. O. would swear the man was
Chinese, a race of which he had an unexplained
terror. The latter fact moves Eliza's attention to
W. O.'s comic, but appalling, display in a
Chinese laundry, where, accompanied by Eliza,
Ben, and Luke, he retrieves his shirts after much
arguing and many threats. W. O. never does produce the much-called-for laundry ticket, to the
frustration of the owner.

A lot of what Eliza tells concerns death: the
Civil War victims; Bill Pentland, who announced the day and hour of his death, turned
his head to the wall and fulfilled his prediction;
W. O.'s first wife, Cynthia, who died of con-
sumption; and the cold-blooded murders com-
mitted by Ed Mears and Lawrence Wayne. This
latter episode includes details of the murderers'
escape from prison, their separation and flight,
and their later days out west. When Mears first

escapes, he comes to the Gants' house, since he has no shoes and only W. O.'s will fit him. Throughout all these tales, Eliza's strength never wavers. She survives the births of children and drunken days of W. O.; she even lectures the murderer Ed Mears so effectively that he hands her his gun before he flees across the mountains.

The structure of the story defies analysis, so intricately are Eliza's tales interconnected. Rereading "The Web of Earth" impresses one with Wolfe's technical skill as well as with the stamina of the protagonist, an old woman who has survived much. The ending unifies the themes of suffering, endurance, and hope when after countless digressions, Eliza finally explains the mysterious words that opened the story: "Two . . . two . . . twenty . . . twenty."[8] These words are a sign of the birth of the twins, Grover and Ben, twenty days after the evening Ed Mears came to beg shoes "at twenty minutes to ten o'clock on the seventeenth of October." (Yet both Grover and Ben, of course, died young.)

Eliza conveys present time by commenting on the sound of the ships in the Brooklyn harbor, and her son must keep pointing out to her the direction of those ships. This setting is new to her, and she has difficulty in getting her bearings. However, she is, in a sense, a compendium of human experience, and she admonishes her son, "My dear child, eat good food and watch and guard your health: it worries me to think of you alone with strangers." She herself has endured a life filled with sadness, loss, and disappointment. Yet when her contemporary, Miller Wright, weighed down with the burdens of the Depression, asks her, "Eliza, what are you going to do?" she says, "Do! . . . I'm going to pitch right in and work till I'm eighty and then . . . I'm goin' to cut loose and *just raise hell!*"[9] Although her optimism is unfailing, the story is filled with tales and recollections that tell of death, despair, and loneliness.

While the pieces in *From Death to Morning* vary sharply in quality and while many are more accurately described as sketches than short stories, Wolfe emerges in this work as "a serious experimenter in fiction" (Holman, *Loneliness*, p. 14). *The Hills Beyond* (1941), the last book from Wolfe's posthumous papers edited and published by Edward Aswell, falls into three parts. First there are ten pieces ranging from two of Wolfe's best short stories ("The Lost Boy" and "Chickamauga") to short sketches such as "No Cure for It," which may have been written, Aswell contends, as early as 1929. The second part, entitled "The Hills Beyond," is a ten-chapter fragment of a novel[10] set in Old Catawba (North Carolina). Although Wolfe goes back as far as September 1593 to relate the setting of the state of Old Catawba (a story similar to that of the Lost Colony in North Carolina), the fragment centers on the patriarch William "Bear" Joyner and his numerous offspring from two marriages. The final portion of the volume is a forty-page note that Edward Aswell wrote about his role as Wolfe's editor. Here Aswell comments on Wolfe's working

habits during the last year of his life as well as
on various pieces included in the volume. Unfortunately, except for the two excellent stories
mentioned above, there is little in *The Hills Beyond* that enhances Wolfe's reputation. However, some critics have seen significance in
Wolfe's returning to the North Carolina mountains for his setting and subject matter and others have praised his detached third-person narration in the novel fragment.

"The Lost Boy," by far the best piece in the
volume, uses the Gant family again and focuses
upon Grover's childhood in Part I, particularly
his initiation experience in the Crockers' candy
store. Paid in postage stamps for work he has
done at Reed's drugstore, Grover, age eleven,
cannot resist the smells of the candy and breaks
his own resolve to stay away from the stingy
Crockers. He goes into the store for 15 cents'
worth of chocolate fudge. His stamps had been
accepted as payment before, but now Crocker
will not refund three one-cent stamps that represent an overpayment. The boy asks for their
return, but he has an inherent respect for his
elders. These old people who run the candy
store are neither plump nor cheerful as such
owners might be expected to be. Their hands
are like bird talons; furthermore, they accuse
Grover of misdealings and threaten to call the
police about the postage stamps. Grover's embarrassment sends him to his father, who
storms from his shop across the street into the
Crockers' store. W. O. throws down the needed
pennies, retrieves the boy's stamps, and delivers
an invective against the Crockers worthy of the

Old Testament prophets: "God has cursed you. He has made you lame and childless as you are—and lame and childless, miserable as you are, you will go to your grave and be forgotten!"

Through the images that begin the story, "light came and went and came again," Wolfe suggests the realization that Grover has come to. Adults, he had thought, are to be respected and depended upon. The Crockers, however, accuse him falsely and humiliate him. Although W. O. rescues him, afterwards he says only "Be a good boy" to a child who has never been anything but good. Grover struggles to regain his sense of reality and looks carefully at his physical surroundings: things are just as they have always been—the square, the fountain, the horse at the water trough, his father's shop. Irrevocable change, however, has come to Grover himself:

But something had gone out of the day, and something had come in again. Out of the vision of those quiet eyes some brightness had gone, and into their vision had come some deeper color. He could not say, he did not know through what transforming shadows life had passed within that quarter hour. He only knew that something had been lost—something forever gained.

What Grover has lost is a great part of his childood innocence; what he has gained is the inevitable experience of the world.

The remaining three parts of this story take place years after Grover's death at age twelve, as the mother, sister, and brother remember Grover and in so doing reveal much about them-

selves. Part II is Eliza's monologue as she talks
to Eugene, telling him again about the trip to
St. Louis long ago. In particular, she relates details about the Fair in St. Louis and remarks on
Grover's maturity and manliness. She coyly recounts how she fooled the reporter from New
Jersey who came to interview her about her famous son, Eugene the novelist. Eliza hinted to
the reporter that Grover, not Eugene, was her
brightest son. Her bragging memories mingle
and reveal much of her past. At the end of this
section, Wolfe returns to the pervasive idea of
time and loss as Eliza says, "It was so long ago,
but when I think of it, it all comes back, as if
it happened yesterday. Now all of you have
either died or grown up and gone away, and
nothing is the same as it was then."

Part III, "The Sister," is Helen's monologue. Like the Ancient Mariner, Eugene's older
sister is compelled to tell her story, and she tells
Eugene about the time in St. Louis that led to
Grover's illness and death. Now in middle age,
Helen realizes that her ambitions are unful-
filled—she will never be a famous singer in an
opera house. Since Eugene has been to college
and reads books, he should have answers to her
questions. What happens, she wants to know,
to all of our expectations and dreams? Wolfe
uses a photograph of the Gant family when they
were young and full of plans to symbolize the
dreams of youth. Helen ponders the photograph; turning to Eugene, she asks, "Does it
happen to us all, to everyone? . . . Grover and
Ben, Steve, Daisy, Luke and me—all standing
there before the house on Woodson Street in

Altamont—there we are, and you see the way we were—and now it all gets lost. What is it, anyway, that people lose?"

Part IV, "The Brother," shows Eugene's attempt to answer Helen's questions. As a grown man, Eugene goes to St. Louis. Working from fragments of childhood memories, he finds the house where the Gants lived during the summer of 1904, the summer of the World's Fair, the summer that Grover died. Inside the house, Eugene peers into a mirror at the bottom of the stairs and momentarily enters the past. He hears Grover's voice, but the recapturing of this childhood experience lasts only for an instant. The "lost boy" of the title is not just Grover, who was lost through death at an early age. It is also Eugene, who learns that one cannot recapture the past save for a fleeting moment. Helen must face the fact that the dreams of childhood often are unrealized; Eugene learns that none of the past can be recaptured, and Helen will learn this too. From all four points of view in this story, Wolfe explores the idea of time and loss and most effectively shows the regret adults have for the past and many of its associations.

"Chickamauga" is the first-person narrative of a Civil War veteran who will be 95 on his next birthday.[11] Although the digressions are not as numerous as Eliza's in "The Web of Earth," several features in these two works are similar. Like Eliza, the old veteran has a remarkable memory. He recalls that, seventy-five years before, on August 7, 1861, "at seven-thirty in the morning . . . I started out from home and walked the whole way to Clingman." There he joined the Twenty-ninth Regiment and headed for battle. Wolfe effectively uses the Civil War as subject matter and renders experience other than his own. The narrator and his friend, Jim Weaver, march off to war; Jim resents every day that keeps him away from home and his love, Martha Patton. Now the old man, Jim's friend so many years ago, describes a day of battle: "The bloodiest fightin' that was ever knowed, until that cedar thicket was soaked red with blood, and thar was hardly a place left in thar where a sparrer could have perched." The narrator describes in homely terms the difficulty of taking Missionary Ridge: it was "like tryin' to swim the Mississippi upstream on a boneyard mule." When Jim Weaver dies in battle, the narrator retrieves from Jim's pockets his watch, his pocket knife, and Martha Patton's letters. Like the sister in "The Lost Boy," the narrator is bewildered at this turn of events: "Hit's funny how hit all turns out—how none of hit is like what we expect." His friend is dead; it is the narrator who lives, goes home, and marries Martha Patton.

In comparison to "The Lost Boy" and "Chickamauga," the remaining stories and sketches in *The Hills Beyond* are slight indeed. "No Cure for It" is a brief sketch about the growing pains of a gangly boy. Here Wolfe revives names from *Look Homeward, Angel*— Eliza, Gant, Dr. McGuire—and the material in this sketch is similar in tone to that first novel. "Gentlemen of the Press," a short piece that was probably written in 1930, uses the devices of a play script to designate speakers, time, and setting. The cub reporter, Red, spins an outlandish tale about Abraham Lincoln being a descendant of Napoleon, and the older men listen with amused tolerance. Red's earnestness is a part of his youth. His ridiculous tale, however, is juxtaposed with reports coming in over the wire services telling of new French casualties in World War I.

"A Kinsman of His Blood" is similar to the Bascom Pentland material in *Of Time and the River*. In this story, Wolfe changes Pentland's name to an earlier version—Bascom Hawke—and tells about one of Bascom's children, who changes his identity and loses touch with reality, talking of nonexistent love affairs. "The Return of the Prodigal" is in two parts: "The Thing Imagined," which is an imagined account by Eugene Gant of his coming home, and "The Real Thing," which is a realistic account of Eugene's return to Altamont. In the second part, Wolfe uses many details of his 1937 trip to Asheville, including a street shooting he witnessed in nearby Burnsville, North Carolina, while he was en route.

The brief sketch "On Leprechauns" belongs to the George Webber material, and "Portrait of a Literary Critic" is Wolfe's satirical picture of the inept type of critic that he loathed. "The Lion at Morning," which belongs to the pre-Depression sections of *You Can't Go Home Again*, portrays James Wyman, Sr., a wealthy banker who begins his day amid routine luxury and unexpected scandal. "God's Lonely Man" is Wolfe's personal anatomy of loneliness.

Aswell suggests that his version went through several drafts and at one point had the title "On Loneliness at Twenty-three."

Besides these stories and sketches, this collection contains the first six chapters of a novel that was to be called by the title Aswell used for the posthumous collection of fragments *The Hills Beyond*. These chapters tell the stories of George Webber's maternal ancestors, the Joyners, whose history begins with William "Bear" Joyner. Wolfe traces the founding of the state, Old Catawba, and particularly satirizes the desire among some of these residents to trace their ancestry:

In the South, particularly, this preoccupation seems to absorb most of the spare energies of the female population for it is an axiom of Southern life that a woman without "family" is nothing. A woman may be poor; she may be abysmally ignorant (and usually is); she may have read nothing, seen nothing, gone nowhere; she may be lazy, nasty, vain, arrogant, venomous, and dishonest; her standards of morality, government, justice may not differ one whit from that of the lynching mob: but if she can assert, loudly and without challenge, that her "family" is older (and therefore better) than other families, then her position in the community is unquestioned, she is the delicate flower of "Southern culture," she must not be "talked back to"—she is, in short, "a lady."

Wolfe's satire includes The Society of the Sons and Daughters of the Aborigines, who would grasp dueling pistols if anyone hinted at a drop of black blood in their ancestry. Just as fervently, however, they claim kin with Indians, "their dusky ancestors of some two and a half centuries before."

William "Bear" Joyner is Wolfe's legendary character, a descendant of Mike Fink, Davy Crockett, and Paul Bunyan, and the Yankee peddler.[12] Extraordinary in every way, Bear founded a large clan. His first wife, Martha Creasman, died in childbirth, and the fates of their surviving children (Zacharias, Hattie, Robert, Theodore, and Rufe) are the primary subject matter of the fragment. Even though Bear's second wife bore him "fourteen or sixteen children . . . there were so many of them, and their destinies were so diverse, that even their number has been disrupted," it is the first set of children who are considered in the narrative. A lawyer like his brother Robert, the colorful Zacharias becomes governor of Old Catawba and later a United States senator. In whatever office he holds, he is generally effective. He exposes social climbers by telling their true history: many have descended from escaped convicts and are themselves people "raised on hawg and hominy." Wolfe perhaps reflects his own distrust of lawyers when he describes them here as "that articulate tribe which was to breed and multiply with such astonishing proliferation during the next century." The assumption that lawyers will enter politics is borne out in Zacharias; however, his brother Robert has no desire to "get into politics." Robert is content to remain a lawyer; his refusing the gains that politics can bring leads people to say that "he was a fine man, of course, but a little queer."

The most elaborate satire in the fragment concerns the brother Theodore. Unable to pass the bar, Theodore marries a "Drumgoole of the Virginia Drumgooles," produces several children, and operates a "military school," the Joyner Heights Military Academy. Zacharias calls Joyner Heights "Hogwart Heights" and derides his brother's every endeavor, especially the pretentious military training provided at the school when the Civil War is imminent. Zack declares that "they had a devil of a time getting those twenty-seven pimply boys straightened up as straight as they could get—which is to say, about as straight as a row of crooked radishes." But when the war comes, those same pimply boys march off and many die. Theodore becomes more foolish after the war. Although he has no legitimate military claim, he is now Colonel Joyner and bears himself, the narrator says, as if "a whole regiment of plumed knights [were] in his own person."

The final four chapters of the fragment center on Robert Joyner, who lost a leg in the Civil War—a fact, that his son Edward learns from a history book. Reading an account of the Battle of Spottsylvania, Edward comes upon the name Joyner in a passage that ends, "among others, I saw Joyner among his gallant mountaineers firing and loading until he was himself shot down and borne away by his own men, his right leg so shattered by a minie ball that amputation was imperative." Bewildered, the boy takes the book to his mother and asks, "What the book says—is that father?" Her answer comes quickly: "Your father is so proud, and in some ways a child himself. He wouldn't tell you. He could not bear to have his son think that his father was a cripple." Now a judge, Robert Joyner is impatient with the old veterans who hang around the courthouse hoping for sympathy. Robert befriends John Webber, a stranger to Libya Hill who arrives with the construction crew of the hotel. Webber's reputation as a fine workman earns him respect, and Wolfe seems to pair him with Robert Joyner, implying that these two men share many of the same good qualities.

The fragment ends with Edward Joyner, now fifty, recalling the day years ago when he discovered that his father had been a Civil War hero. That discovery in turn explains his father's impatience long ago with the hangers on from the war who haunted the courthouse for undeserved sympathy. With Edward's recollection, Wolfe abandons the objective narration that characterizes the fragment and concludes with a meditation on time that is, like so many of Wolfe's lyric passages, quite effective: "And time still passing . . . time passing like river flowing . . . knowing that this earth, this time, this life, are stranger than a dream."

The material in *The Hills Beyond* deserves attention primarily because it shows the variety of writing styles Wolfe tried. But the six chapters of the title fragment are not promising, and certainly the fragment provides no evidence, as some have claimed, that Wolfe's writing had taken a turn away from the autobiographical style of the earlier work.[13] Much material here derives from the folklore tradition and also from

Wolfe's own early work. Furthermore, although satire is prevalent throughout the fragment and in some of the stories, it lacks the power to chastise and reform. Except for making "The Lost Boy" and "Chickamauga" more readily available in this volume, Edward Aswell did little to advance Wolfe's reputation by publishing *The Hills Beyond*, a book that contains much mediocre writing.

In 1961, Scribner's published *The Short Novels of Thomas Wolfe*, a volume edited by C. Hugh Holman, whose introduction and headnotes, along with Wolfe's texts, constitute an indispensable part of the Wolfe canon.[14] Wolfe had difficulty determining what a short story should be, and he agonized over the proper form of a novel. Only a handful of his short stories are first rate, and among his novels only *Look Homeward, Angel* achieves satisfactory form. However, he wrote some of his most successful work in the intermediate-length form of the novella (roughly 20,000 to 30,000 words). In addition to the five short novels in this edition, Holman mentions three others. "The Train and the City," a 12,000-word story, appeared in *Scribner's Magazine* in May 1934. The longer and more successful work "Death the Proud Brother" appeared in the June 1934 issue of the same publication. "Boom Town," which was published in the May 1934 issue of the *American Mercury*, satirizes the real estate craze that swept Asheville before the Depression. Like the previous two works, "Boom Town" was drawn from the large manuscript Wolfe was writing;

furthermore, this long story was the first of Wolfe's work that Elizabeth Nowell placed after she became his agent. The five short novels that Holman edited represent Wolfe's best work except for *Look Homeward, Angel* (see additional discussions of these short novels earlier in this chapter). Each had been published in magazines in the 1930s, and except for "The Web of Earth" all were then placed in various sections of Wolfe's last three novels. At the time, these magazine publications provided a much-needed source of income for Wolfe; indeed, one of the short novels, "A Portrait of Bascom Hawke," tied for the *Scribner's Magazine* short-novel contest. Wolfe split the $5,000 prize with John Herrmann. Based on Wolfe's uncle Henry Westall, Bascom Hawke is Wolfe's most eccentric character. After "A Portrait of Bascom Hawke" appeared in *Scribner's Magazine*, the material it contains was widely dispersed into various sections of *Of Time and the River*. Although the appearance of Bascom in the novel is most interesting, the full short novel presents him, his family, and his co-workers more colorfully and appealingly. The unity gained in the short-novel form was almost totally lost when the work was broken apart.

The longest of the five novellas, "The Web of Earth," appeared in *Scribner's Magazine* in July 1932. When he included this Joycean interior monologue in the collection *From Death to Morning*, Wolfe changed the protagonist's name from Delia Hawke to Eliza Gant and made a few minor additions. Thus, unlike the other titles in the Holman edition of the short novels,

"The Web of Earth" has always been readily available in its original form.

Until the Holman edition appeared, however, "No Door" had never been published in its original four parts, which total some 31,000 words. Since this version was much too long for a single issue, *Scribner's Magazine* published it as two long stories, the first entitled "No Door," and the second "The House of the Far and Lost." Later the first episode of the original version was used as a short story in *From Death to Morning* and "The House of the Far and Lost" was used virtually unchanged in *Of Time and the River*. The remainder of the total 31,000-word version was worked into five sections of *Of Time and the River* and one section of *You Can't Go Home Again*. Without question the discussion of the Coulsons, an English family, is the most interesting part of "No Door." Wolfe presents the alcoholic husband, the wife who gazes out upon the foggy cold weather and declares that in her heart Italy is home, and the daughter, Edith, who in young womanhood resigns herself to a bleak family existence. When Eugene urges Edith to come away with him to America, he declares to her, "Failure and defeat won't last forever." To these words Edith responds, "Sometimes they do." Some secret in the past surrounds this family, but Eugene never learns what it is. Furthermore, he never comes to know his fellow boarders, the three men who squeeze into their small car each day, speed to their factory work, and spend every evening performing American jazz. These men seem compelled to play, yet they do not seem to enjoy the music. The leader, Captain Nicholl, has a mutilated arm; his disfigurement suggests the spiritual wound in the Coulson family. They may be a family that lives beneath a common roof, but each lives a separate life.

The last two short novels in the Holman edition are convincing evidence of Wolfe's growing social awareness and of his ability to write direct, simple, and objective prose. "I have a Thing to Tell You" was Wolfe's awakening to the perils of Nazi Germany.[15] He portrays Berlin no longer as a city of enchantment and friends but instead as a "world hived of four million lives, of hope and fear and hatred, anguish and despair, of love, of cruelty and devotion." Wolfe insisted that this work was not intended as propaganda, and to prevent such accusations he refused to allow a Yiddish translation.

As many critics have pointed out, Wolfe was fortunate that his first publisher had a monthly publication; indeed, *Scribner's Magazine* brought out much of Wolfe's work. His stories and short novels that appeared in this magazine gave Wolfe needed income and kept his name before the reading public, thus enhancing his critical reputation. It was fitting that the May 1939 issue of *Scribner's Magazine* published one of the last pieces Wolfe wrote, "The Party at Jack's," some nine months after Wolfe's death. The editor commented on Wolfe's career and included in the issue's preliminary pages a letter from Max Perkins, who had written, "The credit for Thomas Wolfe belongs to Scribner's if to anyone."[16] Heeding Per-

kins's suggestion, the editor also included a
photograph of the recently completed oil portrait of Wolfe painted by Perkins's son-in-law,
Douglas Gorsline.

"The Party at Jack's" was the last piece of
Wolfe's unpublished work that *Scribner's Magazine* brought out; in the same issue, however,
"An Angel on the Porch" was reprinted with
this editorial note:

Thomas Wolfe's "An Angel on the Porch" was published in the August 1929 issue of *Scribner's Magazine* with these words . . . "The first work of a new
writer about whom much will be heard this fall."
That was almost exactly nine years before Wolfe's
death. We are republishing "An Angel on the Porch"
in this issue as an appropriate companion for "The
Party at Jack's." The first and we are sorry to say,
the last Thomas Wolfe to appear in *Scribner's Magazine.*[17]

Like "I Have a Thing to Tell You," this
final short novel is a statement of strong social
concern written in taut, objective prose. The
reader who assumes that Wolfe's writing was
always lengthy, discursive, and laden with rhetorical devices probably would not guess these
last two short novels to be his work. Wolfe
spent much of the summer of 1937 finishing
"The Party at Jack's"; much of this work was
done while he stayed in a cabin near his Asheville home for several weeks. Holman considers
it one of Wolfe's "most impressive accomplishments" (*Short Novels*, p. xvi).

As previously discussed, the social satire in
"The Party at Jack's" focuses on the absurd per-

formance of Piggy Logan and his circus as well as on the wealthy residents of a luxury Park Avenue apartment building. This short novel also includes Wolfe's invective against pompous literary critics, particularly in the character Seamus Malone. In addition, the action places George Webber in the home of his mistress, Esther Jack. Here he watches her fulfill the roles required of her without ever entirely ignoring him. For George, she is the ideal woman, as appealing in middle age as she is in the portrait painted of her when she was twenty-five. The portrait hangs in Jacks' apartment and during the party several guests comment that both portrait and subject have lasting beauty and grace. Of this George Webber is certain.

Thomas Wolfe did not live to have a second act as a writer; critics continue to speculate whether or not his stylistic excesses might have been curtailed had he continued to write throughout a long life. Although the published corpus is fairly substantial, it is by no means of uniform worth. Wolfe's reputation in the 1980s suffers because his major works are severely flawed. He suffers too because many people, discouraged by the length and the obvious indulgences in style, do not read him, except perhaps for *Look Homeward, Angel*. The charges of egotism, of autobiographical dependence, of rhetorical excess, and of lack of narrative control are made again and again. And although Wolfe's accomplishments are considerable if one evaluates all of his work, most careful readers nevertheless judge him to be a failed artist.

5

"My Name Is Wolfe: I Am an American"

To FULLY EVALUATE Wolfe, it is important to be aware of the range of narrative techniques Wolfe employed and to judge their success. Certainly he was influenced by Joyce's experimentation in *Ulysses*, which led him, for example, to employ sound devices, word play, and stream-of-consciousness techniques. The broad scope of his work, his attempts to hear and see and tell everything, accounts for his use of varying stylistic methods. Although he used conventional devices—similes, metaphors, images, symbols, allusions—in conventional ways, his style is nonetheless highly individual. His individuality is, however, unfortunately marred by his self-indulgent rhetoric.

Many techniques were successful. For example, Wolfe, a compulsive listener, reproduced speech accurately: pronunciation, regional accents, and conversational patterns. His purpose was often to use speech to represent a character fully. At times, however, Wolfe implicitly satirized characters by their manner of speaking. Wolfe knew the Brooklyn dialect well and he frequently wrote in it. Used especially effectively in "Only the Dead Know Brooklyn," this dialect conveys the consternation the Brooklyn native expresses about a stranger who thinks he can get to know Brooklyn by following a map. With the map, the man insists, he will not get lost. The Brooklyn native's speech reveals his narrow outlook and suggests a less-educated background than that of the outsider whose faith in the map suggests his trust in reason and order. The native thinks:

A map! Red Hook! Jesus!

So den duh guy begins to ast me all kinds of nutty questions: how big was Brooklyn an' could I find my way aroun' in it, an' how long would it take a guy to know duh place. "Listen," I says. "You get dat idea outa yoeh head right now," I says. "You ain't neveh gonna get to know Brooklyn," I says. "Not in a hundred yeahs. I been livin' heah all my life," I says, "an' I don't even know all deh is to know about it, so how do you expect to know duh town," I says, "when you don't even live heah?"

The reported conversation never gets beyond this impasse because the men do not realize their different methods of *knowing* Brooklyn.

Though he was no linguist or dialectician, Wolfe exercised care in presenting speech patterns. For instance, when he was finishing the revisions of "I Have a Thing to Tell You," he wrote to Elizabeth Nowell that he was "worried about a lot of things—phonetics, accents, etc. I'm not yet sure what to do about all the 'zis,' 'zese,' 'zem' business. . . . If you think best, make it consistent—that is, get all the 'th' words consistent: 'fazzer,' 'mozzer,' 'zis,' 'zat,' etc. The character I had in mind really did not speak with such a marked or broken accent; yet he *did* have an accent and I had to suggest it somehow."[1] Another speech distinction present in the novels is the Boston accent, which Wolfe showed by the pronunciation of words such as "strangeh," "otheh," and "wahm bed." The British accent especially intrigued him. In far too much detail in *Of Time and the River*, he analyzes a vicar's accent as an English family listens to him after dinner. They are discussing Goldsmith's *The Vicar of Wakefield*; "vicar" comes out as "vicah," "years" as "yöhs," and "extraordinary" as "straw'n'ry."

Wolfe also successfully conveyed the banalities of the American tourist in Europe. In "One of the Girls in Our Party," the Midwestern schoolteacher says, "Why the *prices* are just aw-w-ful! . . . I'd always heard how cheap it was, but after *this*!—you can't tell me!" Wolfe describes such tourists' voices as nasal, complaining, whining; voices of the European officials are brusque, hurried, impatient. Affected speech characterizes Jerry Alsop (*The Web and the Rock*); when he says "Mothah," the narrative voice comments: "It can be said without exaggeration that it represented the final and masterly conquest of the vocal chords, beside which such efforts, say, as those of the late Senor Caruso striking the high C seem fairly paltry by comparison." Eugene considers his students inept because they say "Keiths" for Keats, "Wadsworth" for Wordsworth. To Wolfe and Eugene, how a person speaks often reveals what a person is.

Of Time and the River has a short episode in which Wolfe lets a character revel in meaningless abstractions. Dr. Thornton, a retired physician living at the Hotel Leopold, says to her fellow residents: "'I see nothing but order and harmony in the universe. I lift my eyes unto the stars,' . . . at the same time lifting her face in a movement of rapturous contemplation toward the ceiling of the hotel lobby." She continues a rhapsody about the noble creature, man; however, her audience is composed of commonplace guests and workers, who embody few, if any, noble attributes. In another episode, a newspaper reporter calls in a story about a Park Avenue fire. Exasperated by the night clerk's limited vocabulary, the reporter shouts, "Cordon, I say! C-o-r-d-o-n! . . . How long have you been working on a newspaper, anyway? Didn't yuh ever hear of a cordon before?" Apparently the night clerk never had, and Wolfe implies that with the word "cordon" the reporter is overwriting.

It is true that Wolfe often patterned his later characters on earlier ones, and speech patterns are a primary clue to this. For example, Aunt Maw (*The Web and the Rock*) talks like Eliza Gant, as does Delia Hawke (*You Can't Go Home Again*). When Aunt Maw's servant fails to appear one morning, she complains, "To think that fool nigger—I could wring her neck when I think of it—well, as I say now . . . here I was depending on her—and I'm left here in the lurch." Eliza Gant complained in similar words and in a similar tone when she was left at Dixieland with no help. (Eliza, after all, was often stingy and slow with wages.) These women represent, of course, a Southern type: the hard-working, put-upon woman who endure the trials of life, including incompetent servants. Another device Wolfe uses effectively is associating particular words or expressions with specific characters. Eliza's expression "Pshaw, now!" is her most frequent exclamation and her clairvoyant moments are introduced with "I just had a feeling. I don't know what you'd call it." To this line and to many others, W. O.'s response is, "Jesus God! . . . It's begun again." Luke Gant stutters ("You m-m-m-miserable d-d-d-degenerate"), and Helen's voice far too often has "its old cracked note of hysteria." When Eudora Welty gives readings from *Losing Battles*, she tells audiences not to bother with keeping the individual voices straight. Better, she says, to consider them as a chorus. Indeed, the members of the Beecham family in *Losing Battles* do seem to speak as one. But the members of the Gant family do not, and neither do any other groups of characters in Wolfe's fiction. These characters are highly individual and often antagonistic toward each other; their voices are singular.

Certainly one of Wolfe's most successful techniques, especially in *Look Homeward,*

Angel, is burlesque. The description of the woman who rents part of Gant's house after Eliza opens the boarding house is a good example: "A grass widow, forty-nine, with piled hair of dyed henna, corseted breasts and hips architecturally protuberant in a sharp diagonal, meaty mottled arms, and a gulched face of leaden flaccidity puttied up mightily with cosmetics, rented the upstairs of Woodson Street while Helen was absent." The effect is comic even if the modifiers are exaggerated and the tone farcical.

Among Wolfe's least successful devices are his hyphenated modifiers, numerous present participles, and unconventional adjectives. A single page from *Look Homeward, Angel* provides these examples: "A great tree of birds will sing . . . burgeoning richly, filling the air also with warm-throated plum-drooping birdnotes"; and "the harsh hill-earth." These modifiers occur frequently, but never more so than in these passages: "The stilted Cadillac gasped cylindrically up the hill." Eugene drops his nickel in the Sunday school collection plate "since he usually had enough left over for cold gaseous draughts at the soda fountain." These passages are unnecessarily fancy for a car climbing a steep slope and a boy buying a 5¢ soda.

By means of elevated diction and inverted syntax (usually placing subjects after verbs or modifiers after nouns), Wolfe sometimes ascribes extraordinary qualities to ordinary events. For instance, when Eliza Gant awakens early at Dixieland, the description suggests that a goddess has awakened: "Roofing the deep tides, swinging in their embrace, rocked Eliza's life Sargassic, as when, at morning, a breath of kitchen air squirmed through her guarded crack of door, and fanned the pendant clusters of old string in floating rhythms." The verb precedes the subject; an unusual adjective follows the noun—"rocked Eliza's life Sargassic." Air "squirms" (a word out of keeping with the remaining diction), and an ordinary bedroom door is cracked but "guarded." The old string that Eliza compulsively saves is here not just a dust catcher. Instead, it becomes "pendant clusters" that fan about in the air. Many other such examples illustrate these traits, which are often the result of simply hasty or careless writing. But the early morning scene at Dixieland shows Wolfe could use them successfully: "into the April night-and-morning streets goes Ben"; an "orchard stirs leafily"; and "lazily slaps the water in the fountain on the Square."

Detail is the means by which a writer fixes a character's face, brings to life the sight of a holiday table, or makes memorable the individual sounds of human voices. Although Wolfe is at times too profuse with details, he usually selects those that are apt. His success comes in part from his almost total recall (a trait his mother also possessed). Furthermore, he was a careful observer. Repeatedly in his notebooks he sketched hands, building spires, and faces—details he had remembered. He was unusually adept at using details of clothing to reveal characters' personalities. For example, Jim Trivett's clothing shows the fashion at Pulpit Hill—at least the fashion of a country boy come to col-

lege. The son of a rich tobacco farmer, Trivett's
unruly hair, tobacco-juice stains, and bad teeth
contrast sharply with his all-American college
man dress, circa 1920: "Skin-tight trousers
. . .[which] ended an inch above his oxford shoes
exposing an inch of clocked hose, a bobtailed
coat belted in across the kidneys, large striped
collars of silk. Under his coat he wore a big
sweater with high-school numerals."

Clothing details are also important in de-
scribing Eugene's fellow workers in the Norfolk
shipyards. Many of the workers are Georgia
farm boys who have never before earned ten,
twelve, or eighteen dollars a day. At night, these
same boys appear on the streets dressed extrav-
agantly in "$18.00 leathers, $80.00 suits, and
$8.00 silk shirts with broad alternating bands
of red and blue." This same garish taste is presented in *The Web and the Rock* in the vivid
picture of the dreary part of Libya Hill, the Doubleday section. Here boys have harsh names;
become hobos, pool-room loafers, pimps, or bul-
lies who live off whores; and wear "cheap-look-
ing, flashy clothes, bright yellow, box-toed
shoes, and loud-striped shirts, suggesting somehow an unwholesome blending of gaudy finery
and bodily filth."

Ironically, in spite of having more money
than most other Altamont citizens, Eliza Gant
rarely wears becoming clothes. Indeed, she dons
her bargaining outfit when she buys and sells
real estate, seeing a distinct advantage in not
dressing too well when trading. Even at home,
where she nags everyone to turn off lights to
economize, she wears shabby sleepwear. The

narrative voice describes her as "clothed in a tattered old sweater and indefinable underlappings." In contrast, Laura James dresses "elegantly in short plaid skirts and waists of knitted silk." The family of Joel Pierce and their Hudson River neighbors pay much attention to dressing properly: gentlemen *will* wear white flannels. But Wolfe's most elegantly dressed character is Francis Starwick. Clothes not only mark Starwick as a poseur but also are one means of revealing to Eugene that Starwick is homosexual. On the steps of the Louvre Eugene by chance meets Starwick, "wearing a Russian blouse of soft blue wool which snuggled around his neck in voluptuous folds and had a kind of diamond-shaped design of crimson threads along the band." Still carrying and indolently twirling his cane, Starwick is "elegantly dressed, as always, in casual, beautifully tailored, brown tweed garments."

And clothing details figure in one of Eugene Gant's most frustrating moments. He had ordered a suit to be made, but when he went for a fitting he found that the suit

was vilely botched and skimped, sufficient cloth had not been put into it, and now it was too late to remedy the defect. Yet, the fitter gravely pulled the vest down till it met the trousers, tugged at the coat, and pulled the things together where it stayed until Eugene took a breath or moved a muscle, when it would all come apart again, the collar bulging outward from the shoulder, the skimpy coat and vest crawling backward from the trousers, leaving a hiatus of shirt and belly that could not now be remedied by any means.

In spite of the obvious and irremediable flaws in the suit, the tailor murmurs, "Um! Seems to fit you very well." Details convey the humor: "collar bulging outward," "coat and vest crawling backward," "a hiatus of shirt and belly."

Wolfe's most extensive use of detail, however, is the catalogue. Because he liked its inclusiveness, he used frequently: catalogues of odors, boats, American cities, occupations, vagrants' names, sports, farm products, flowers, mountain towns and gaps and gorges, sounds, authors' names, book titles, Altamont citizens, window displays, and, above all, foods. Except Whitman, few American writers have used the catalogue as extensively or as effectively as Wolfe. One illustration concerns Eliza's numerous belongings, which, the narrative voice says, possessed her "like the desperate clutch of life itself." She clings to everything she ever owned: "old bottles, papers, pieces of string, worn-out gloves with all the fingers missing, frayed cast-off sweaters which some departed boarder had left behind him, postcards, souvenirs, seashells, coconuts, old battered trunks, dilapidated furniture which could no longer be used, calendars for the year 1906, showing coy maidens simpering sidewise out beneath the crisply ruffled pleatings of a Japanese parasol—a mountainous accumulation of old junk for which the old dilapidated house had now become a fit museum."

Throughout his writing, Wolfe never tires of cataloguing food—its appearance, aroma, and taste. He cites the particulars of holiday feasts,

huge breakfasts, gourmet meals prepared by Esther Jack for George Webber, the fare in cafes
and restaurants at home and abroad, extravagant tea tables, vegetable gardens in season, and
abundant orchards. The description of the
kitchen at the Pierces' Hudson River estate illustrates the detail Wolfe provided when a
kitchen, dining room, or restaurant is needed
for the ritual of eating. Here he begins with general categories of foods kept in ordinary con-
tainers, moves to specific fruits and vegetables,
then lists exotic condiments, and finally names
foods with pungent odors:

There was food in cans, and food in tins, and food
in crocks, and food in bottles. There were—in addition to such staple products of the canning art as
corn, tomatoes, beans and peas, pears, plums and
peaches, such rarer relishes as herrings, sardines, ol-
ives, pickles, mustard, relishes, anchovies. There
were boxes of glacéd crystalline fruits from California, and little wickered jars of sharp-spiced ginger
fruit from China; there were expensive jellies green
as emerald, red as rubies, smoother than whipped
cream, there were fine oils and vinegars in bottles,
and jars of pungent relishes of every sort, and boxes
of assorted spices. . . . A haunting and nostalgic fu-
sion of delicious smells whose exact quality it is impossible to define, but which has in it the odors of
cinnamon, pepper, cheese, smoked ham, and cloves.

After noting this profusion, Eugene opens the
great door of the icebox, and for two pages Wolfe
describes its contents, which will furnish Eugene with what his host calls "a snack."
   Wolfe had several motives for devoting this

large number of pages to food catalogues and descriptions. First, Wolfe uses precise descriptions of food and its selection as a means of revealing characters' backgrounds. In *Look Homeward, Angel*, for example, the Gants' bountiful table bears food that the middle class would normally have. Indeed, in most Southern households, figs, raisins, mixed nuts, and Florida fruits are associated with holidays, not with everyday menus. Such foods are "auxiliary dainties," and "strange foods and fruits" that arrive in the grocer's boxes a few days before celebrations. Although Joel Pierce's mother is Southern and sometimes serves dishes Eliza's boarders would have expected, Mrs. Pierce's kitchen regularly stocks anchovies, Austrian hams, and herrings. Esther Jack carefully shops for the tenderest lettuces, the freshest vegetables, the best meats. The meals she prepares for George Webber are an emblem of their courtship. And Thomas Wolfe declared once that he himself had eaten more T-bone steaks and baked potatoes than anybody else in America.

Another writing technique that Wolfe used was the imitation of sounds and rhythms. It is the sound of the train that he often used, as in the opening of *Of Time and the River*. Here, violent coupling and sudden movements are conveyed through onomatopoeic words written in upper-case letters: "WHAM! SMASH!" Once the train is moving along at a fast clip, the sounds fall into variations of repetitive nonsense patterns: "Click, clack, clackety-clack . . . stip, step, rackety-rack." Action verbs personify the train's movements and sounds: "rock, smash, swerve . . . let her whir-r, and let her pur-r, at eighty per-r!" The calmness that comes when the ride is well underway produces a different set of sounds in the night. As the train passes through the Virginia countryside, Wolfe introduces the rhythmic phrase, "dreaming in the moonlight." He then repeats the phrase several times but varies the participle by using "beaming," "seeming," "gleaming," and "streaming." The passage ends with the song-like repetition of "—Mo—hoo-oolight-oolight oolight oonlight oonlight oonlight . . . —To be seeming to be dreaming in the moonlight!" As the night draws to a close and the train nears the Baltimore station, Wolfe introduces the personifications Pale Pity and Lean Death, who forever keep time with the train. Now sounds and rhymes of Latin words are used to end the whole sequence. The passage of fifty-odd Latinate words must be heard for its full effect; however, it illustrates visually Wolfe's experiments in suggesting the sounds of the train.

Word play deteriorates in *You Can't Go Home Again* when the narrative voice praises Foxhall Edwards (Max Perkins's fictional counterpart), declaring that Edwards is not numbered among the joiners and fashion apes. Edwards "was none of your like franky-panky, jolasy-wolasy, cowley-wowley, tastesty-wastesy, hicksey-icksey, wilsony-pilsony, . . . sneer-puss fellows." Nothing redeems this passage; one can only regret that Wolfe did not drop it and others like it at an early stage.

Occasionally, Wolfe uses sentence length

to indicate a character's temperament or background. For example, at the end of Chapter 7 of
Look Homeward, Angel, W. O. Gant returns to
Altamont from a long trip. As he builds up the
kitchen fire before waking his household, he
mutters to himself in "his carefully punctuated
rhetoric." His 106-word sentence catalogues his
travels; the river image parallels his rich rest-
less, life, which is somewhat alien to his family.
In this sentence the process of association
works as Gant recalls places, odors, people, and
slightly sensual memories of women:

Yes, musty cotton, baled and piled under long sheds
of railway sidings; and odorous pine woodlands of
the level South, saturated with brown faery light,
and broken by the tall straight leafless poles of trees;
a woman's leg below an elegantly lifted skirt mount-
ing to a carriage in Canal Street (French or Creole
probably); a white arm curved reaching for a window
shade, French-olive faces window-glimmering, the
Georgia doctor's wife who slept above him going out,
the unquenchable fishfilled abundance of the un-
fenced, blue, slow cat-slapping lazy Pacific; and the
river, the all-drinking, yellow, slow-surging snake
that drained the continent.

The inclusiveness of this sentence partially suggests W. O. Gant's life: his travels and his
women.

Less effective long sentences (many contain
more than 200 words) occur in *You Can't Go
Home Again* when Foxhall Edwards reads *The
New York Times* and ruminates about the various news items. On the other hand, short sentences are often used effectively in Wolfe's

work. When he describes Judge Rumford Bland in *You Can't Go Home Again*, Wolfe begins with the sentence "But he was stained with evil." The simple declaration is then elaborated in longer and longer sentences until the insidious web of Bland's evil dealings as usurer has been set out. Another example is the dowdy group bound for Charleston in *Look Homeward, Angel* who are presented in short, choppy sentences. The sentences' verbs are as lifeless as the characters: "The other girl, Louise, was a waitress. She was small, plump, a warm brunette. Mrs. Bowden was a sallow woman with ratty brown hair. She had brown worn-out eyes. She was a dressmaker. Her husband, a carpenter, had died in the Spring. There was a little insurance money. That was how she came to take the trip." Immediately following this passage, the narrative voice returns to varied, rhythmic sentences, rich with description and vivid verbs: "dozed," "wailed," "bedded," "paraded."

Wolfe's rhetorical questions are numerous ("Who has seen fury riding in the mountain?"); he uses personifications freely; he intersperses Latin, Greek, French, and German words; he quotes stanzas and tag lines from songs and poems; he writes daydreams, parodies, and burlesques. Any one of his four novels contains all these techniques; all four display his overindulgence as well as his lyricism, that characteristic of his best writing.[2] For example, the stream-of-consciousness section that begins Chapter 10 of *Of Time and the River* has a lyrical quality as well as a series of mental associations triggered by familiar poem and song tags. The setting is Arles, France. Seated in a cafe, Eugene ruminates upon time; each mental association produces another, and all these memories relate to the word "time." Eugene begins the section with tag lines from "A Game of Chess" in *The Waste Land*. He alludes to (but does not accurately quote) Eliot's "Hurry up please it's time": "Time, please, time . . . Time Gentlemen." The word "time" prompts him to recite Shakespeare's line, "That time of year thou mayst in me behold." After the allusion to the sonnet, the association leaps to time as mentioned in the popular song: "In the good old summer-time." Next the narrative voice says, "A long time ago the world began"; with this line the past comes to life through Eugene's memory of Eliza's daily urging the children to get to school: "Run: you'll just have time." Immediately following her words comes another song tag—"There are times that make you ha-a-ap-py, there are times that make you sa-a-ad." These memories of school, time, and death coalesce as Eugene recalls the night at Pulpit Hill when, just returned from Ben's funeral and deeply grieved, he talks with a classmate. For Eugene, the sense of time and loss is intense. This section ends with the word "well," and memory moves from Eugene as a college student back to his early boyhood with Eliza's words, "It's time all little boys were in bed."

In the next part of this sequence, Eliza speaks. The time is the present, and she attempts to date a former event. It occurred, she now remembers, when W. O. made his trip to

California in 1906. Mention of W. O. and 1906 triggers the memory of four former presidents— Garfield, Arthur, Harrison, and Hayes. These names sadden W. O., for they are all long dead, and in their deaths he seems to see his own: "I knew them all," he says. "By God, I'm getting old." Eliza's voice is heard for a final time, recounting the birth of Grover and Ben the year the locusts stripped bare every tree. (This is an episode Wolfe uses again in "The Web of Earth.") Like W. O., Eliza recognizes lost time and ends her passage with words of resignation: "So much has happened, and it seems so long ago." This entire episode centers now on Eugene, who remembers the inscription on his watch, Ben's gift for his twelfth birthday. A watch, Eugene says, is "to keep time with"; but death is the one thing that time cannot arrest or keep. Eugene closes the episode with his poetic lament for Ben: "Up on the mountain, down in the valley, deep, deep in the hill, Ben, cold, cold, cold."

Yet another remarkably fine passage is Chapter 14 of *Look Homeward, Angel*, in which Wolfe describes early morning in Altamont. Beginning with Ben, who leaves the house at 3:25 A.M. for his newspaper job, Wolfe travels through the dark streets showing various people waking up to the new day. First are newspaper men, doctors, and all-night-cafe operators—all part of nighttime in America. Then, other people are introduced. At 6:10 A.M., Gant wakes up, as do others: Judge Webster Tayloe, Eliza, Dixieland boarders, and the Presbyterian minister, Dr. H. J. McRae. All are in different places; all have different needs. Without comment, Wolfe describes the body of a black thief, Moses Andrews. He lies behind the fence boarding on upper Valley Street; his death contrasts sharply with the lives of the others. Next, Wolfe mentions a poker party that has just broken up at the Altamont City Club. The players go out into the daylight as local businesses open for the day. A young newspaper carrier, who began his route before daylight, now steps into the waiting bedroom of May Corpening in Niggertown.

In this passage, Wolfe includes people of many social classes, suggests the disparity between the public and private lives of many, and realistically describes some three dozen characters. Throughout the passage, Wolfe keeps time in the foreground. The reader has watched Altamont from 3:25 A.M. until daylight has fully come and most of the town's citizens have begun a new day.

Wolfe usually made good use of contemporary allusions which add reality to his fiction. For instance, William Jennings Bryan visits Altamont, and in New York, Joel Pierce's mother visits her Hudson River neighbors, the Franklin Roosevelts. On other occasions Wolfe uses the actual names of prize fighters, baseball players (a sport he loved and followed all his life), writers, literary critics, and political and business officials. Such names and details convey much about the 1920s and 1930s that would have been featured in every city newspaper at the time.

Perhaps more interesting are Wolfe's literary allusions, which he uses for many purposes, often comic. In *Look Homeward, Angel*, when a milliner with the pedestrian name of Mrs. Thelma Jarvis drains her soda glass at the drugstore fountain, the narrator says, "Drink to me only with thine eyes," a poetic suggestion Thelma would not understand. As she leaves, making her way through the crowded tables, the narrator quotes a startling line from Donne's poem, "The Canonization": "For God's sake, hold your tongue and let me love!" Certainly neither Thelma nor the other customers would understand this injunction. Allusions to paintings occur frequently, too, usually to Wolfe's favorite artists—Hogarth, Brueghel, van Gogh, Cranach, Grünewald, Turner. Musical allusions, however, do not appear often, and opera was usually a source of satire for Wolfe. For example, in *Of Time and the River*, Wolfe explains the homosexual Starwick's aberrant behavior as "fitting only in a world of opera." In *The Web and the Rock* Esther includes in her childhood recollections for George Webber a story about going to the opera: "It was one of those operas of Wagner's, and you know how everybody gets killed in them, and we were coming up the aisle just before the end and Uncle Bob came booming out, 'They're all dead except the orchestra!' . . . god! I thought they'd have to stop the show." It does not matter which of Wagner's operas is alluded to here: the response is uninformed, melodramatic, unrealistic, and silly. Wolfe lets Esther Jack make a simplistic judgment that in real life Aline Bernstein doubtless would not have made. One does

not have to like opera to consider it as a serious
art form. Wolfe, however, was seldom seriously
interested in music.

Unquestionably, Wolfe "had a real touch
for comic exaggeration."[3] For example, he
writes daydreams in which Eugene Gant imagines himself as hero and rescuer, calling himself
"Bruce-Eugene" and "the Dixie Ghost." In such
roles he projects himself as the stereotypic he-
roes of dime novels. Similarly, an elaborate sequence in *The Web and the Rock* has George
Webber imagining that he finds an evening bag
in Central Park. When he finds the rich young
widow who lost it, she promptly falls in love
with him. The imaginary conversation of these
two is the stuff of soap opera, but the daydreams
are effective satires on the excesses of youth
that Eugene, George—and probably Wolfe himself—display. The daydream characters are
amusing: the rich young widow, for example,
has an incongruous assemblage of magazines in
her library; *The Police Gazette* stands beside
Punch and *Harper's Weekly*. Furthermore, the
young hero is a writer who declares that after
the success of his first book, "he would own no
property save a small lodge with thirty acres of
woodland, upon a lake in Maine or New Hamp-
shire." No one knew better than Wolfe that first
novels are hard to get published and may not
earn their authors enough to buy one acre, much
less thirty and a lodge.

The effectiveness of Wolfe's exaggerated
humor is also evident in other scenes. Among
the best examples from *Look Homeward, Angel*
is the funeral parlor scene with the obsequious

undertaker, Horse Hines. Other moments of comedy are Mr. Leonard's bumbling attempts to teach Latin and German and Eugene's outrageous appearance as Prince Hal during the Altamont Shakespeare celebration.[4] Finally, a prime example of successful comedy in Wolfe's work involves a vivid description of Luke Gant, the salesman:

He was a hustler: he sold patent washboards, trick potato-peelers, and powdered cockroach-poison from house to house. To the negroes he sold hair-oil guaranteed to straighten kinky hair, and religious lithographs, people with flying angels, white and black, and volant cherubs, black and white, sailing about the knees of an impartial and crucified Saviour, and subtitled, "God Loves Them Both." They sold like hot cakes.

Wolfe could be, and he often was, a writer whose style was completely under control.

Many of Wolfe's attitudes toward life and the role of the artist can be ascertained through his letters and notebooks and, to an extent, documented through his fiction. His autobiographical identification with Eugene Gant and George Webber is obvious, and often these characters are obsessed with the same ideas and issues that concerned Wolfe. Wolfe celebrated America's cities and towns, people and their occupations, rivers and mountains and plains. However, the frantic desire of Americans to achieve quick fortunes appalled him. Long before the boom in Asheville real estate, Wolfe decried to Margaret Roberts people who showed

"greed, greed, greed—deliberate, crafty, moti-
vated—masked under the guise of civic association for municipal betterment." He de-
spaired because "the standards of national
greatness are Henry Ford, who made automo-
biles cheap enough for all, and money, money,
money!! And Thomas A. Edison, who gave us
body-ease and comfort" (Letters, p. 33). When
fortunes in Asheville collapsed during the
Depression, Wolfe remembered his mother's
theory about wealth: it took, she declared, three
generations from shirt sleeves to shirt sleeves.
The acute suffering during the Depression is reflected in Wolfe's depiction of people who cannot escape poverty. Some end up as hobos and
bums; some are black and have little chance in
the white man's world; others are ignorant and
have little hope of education.

The plight of the underprivileged and the
poor was a real issue for Wolfe, and he abhorred
the easy solutions offered by do-gooders, such
as the president of Pine Rock College in The
Web and the Rock. The president urges his students to serve the community by living righ-
teously; however, his efforts have made no im-
provement among the needy of the state. In that
region, children still work fourteen hours a day
in cotton mills, adults are exploited as tenant
farmers, and one million blacks have no vote
and no education. Nevertheless, the narrator reports, class after class graduates from Pine Rock
College with high ideals and goes forth "to de-
fend monogamy, matrimony, pure sweet
women, children, the Baptist Church, the Con-

stitution, the splendid ideals of the Democratic and Republican parties." Wolfe's letters in the 1930s recorded his distress over seeing the poor huddled in subway stations, on park benches, and in the doorways of stores. These people were defenseless against the weather and the Depression.

Like so many families in Asheville and throughout the country, Wolfe's own people lost practically everything when Asheville's Central Bank failed in November 1930. Never insensitive to suffering, Wolfe sent his family as much money as he could. He agreed with his sister Mabel that most of the country's money was in New York; however, he pointed out to her that "our 'Prosperity' is a very uneven thing. There are a great many rich and well-to-do people, but there are millions who just make enough to skin through on. Most of the people in New York are like this—scraping by, with nothing left over" (*Letters*, p. 179).

Wolfe was disturbed by superficial people who considered membership in civic and social clubs tantamount to success. From New York he wrote Mabel that he occasionally saw an Asheville paper and what he read there led him to believe a club existed "for everything under the sun, including hog raising." He added, "I don't blame you for letting some of the club work go" (*Letters*, p. 179). In dealing with this problem in *Look Homeward, Angel*, Wolfe questions phases of "the American dream." Not as vituperative as Sinclair Lewis in satirizing America's middle-class life, Wolfe does scorn

much in Altamont and Asheville. He has Helen
Gant confess that she has pushed her husband
Hugh and herself

until now he belongs to the Rotary Club, and I belong
to the Thursday Literary Club, the Orpheus Society,
the Saturday Musical Club, the Woman's Club, the
Discussion Group, and God knows what else—all
these silly and foolish little clubs in which we have
no interest—and yet it would kill us if we did not
belong to them, we feel that they are a sign that we
are "getting ahead." Getting ahead to what?

Pressure to join clubs is to be sure a less significant problem than the frantic acquisition of
property or the fight to survive the Depression.
Nevertheless, trivial social concerns and getting
rich quick are aspects of American life that
alarmed Wolfe. Although he did speak at one
meeting of a civic organization when he returned to Asheville in 1937, Wolfe himself was
no joiner or accumulator. Indeed, he never
owned a car or property outright. Such things
were not measures of success in his judgment.

Wolfe's social awareness was also affected
by Nazi Germany. The terror he witnessed in
1936 was an emotional and intellectual turning
point in his life. During the difficult years of
the Depression and the impending political
chaos for Germany and all of Europe, he was
responsive to the distress of friends, strangers,
and nations, even though he was not a political
activist. Like his character George Webber,
Wolfe "reached maturity late, but the significant fact—and one frequently overlooked—is
that he did achieve a maturity of social thinking

as the center of his interest shifted near the end of his life from the individual to the society which shapes the individual."[5]

Wolfe was the contemporary of Scott Fitzgerald and Ernest Hemingway, all three of whom had Max Perkins as their editor. Wolfe, however, shunned the life-styles of his two fellow novelists. Indeed, any hint of expatriation irked Wolfe, as did the barren-earth, dry-bones attitude of those who played out themes from Eliot's *The Waste Land*. He despised the poseur, the dilettante, the pseudo-intellectual, as well as insensitive literary critic and ridicules such people in letters and in fiction. For example, the critic Ernest Boyd, as Seamus Malone in *You Can't Go Home Again*, dismisses James Joyce, declaring to the cocktail-party listeners, "Oh, I suppose there is some slight talent there—some minor vestiges, at any rate. Strictly speaking, of course, the fellow is a school-teacher—a kind of pedant who should be teaching the sixth form somewhere in a Jesuit Seminary. . . . He has *something*—not a great deal, but something." Equally irritating to Wolfe were the rich and fashionable people who form their opinions about books after they have read what "in" reviewers say.[6] Although Wolfe himself behaved badly in public from time to time when he had drunk too much, he was a forthright man. The hypocrisy of others was quickly apparent to him.

As a writer, Wolfe worked long, hard hours. Indeed, Edward Aswell said Wolfe worked harder than he ever saw anybody else work.[7] Throughout his last year in New York, Wolfe

conferred with Aswell twice a week and saw
Elizabeth Nowell regularly, but he rarely saw
anyone socially. His routine was to rise about
11:00, have breakfast, and start writing. A sec-
retary came at noon to take dictation or to type
the manuscript he had ready; she left around
6:00. He worked steadily until he stopped for
dinner at around 9:00. Although he took vaca-
tions when his nerves could no longer tolerate
the pressure, Wolfe was seldom away from his
work for long periods. His method of composing
was unusual: in 1935, when he began dictating,
his various secretaries were surprised at the finished quality of the material he dictated. Wolfe
explained that previously he had mentally written the sequences and then rewritten them. The
rigorous work schedule and the meticulous care
he took in rewriting and revising contradict the
idea that Wolfe was an undisciplined writer.
Clearly, he could discipline himself to a rigid
and demanding daily schedule. His great problem was that he let his style go out of control
and then had difficulty in the final stages when
cutting and condensing were demanded. When
he finished a piece, he had difficulty letting go
of it. He once wrote Elizabeth Nowell that
when manuscript pages should be sent to an editor, "a kind of paralysis sets in, I won't get them
typed, I won't send them out, and once a publisher gets anything I write into proofs, I become
more and more reluctant, . . . I keep the proofs
until they are taken from me" (*Letters*, p. 326).

Nothing disrupted Wolfe's rigorous schedule more than the lawsuits he was involved in
during the late 1930s. The threat of libel had

existed even before *Look Homeward, Angel* was published. In 1925, Wolfe wrote to Margaret Roberts about "Passage to England," a travel piece he thought about sending to the Asheville *Citizen*. He planned a subtitle, "Log of a Voyage That Was Never Made," because it would be "a device to escape libel" (*Letters*, p. 95). Once *Look Homeward, Angel* appeared, Wolfe was open to libel and defamation of character suits, but "despite all the opportunities, no Ashevillian has ever brought suit against Wolfe and the *Angel*."[8] However, a troublesome time for Wolfe did occur when Marjorie Dorman, portrayed as Mad Maude in "No Door," sued him in December 1936. By February 1937, Scribner's persuaded Wolfe to settle out of court so that he could get his attention back on his work. (Wolfe's part of the settlement, $2,745.25, was paid by Scribner's out of his royalties [*Letters*, p. 610].) Less costly in money was Wolfe's last court suit, his own case against Murdoch Dooher, an agent who had mishandled sales and then refused to return Wolfe's manuscripts. Wolfe's victory was a great relief, and the occasion brought Wolfe and Max Perkins together for the last time. (Perkins had been a witness.) After court, they went out together. Years later, Perkins frequently expressed his regret that a rare-book dealer had also gone with them. The man's presence kept Perkins and Wolfe from talking as they had in former days.

In addition to these court cases, Wolfe had a dispute with Madeleine Boyd over her sale of the German rights to his work and over her claim for a commission on his work after *Look*

Homeward, Angel. While Wolfe was vindicated in several of these legal matters, he was a man who inevitably got into such difficulties. Elizabeth Nowell appends a note to the *Letters* recounting a 1923 episode that shows Wolfe's tendency to engage in legal battle. He had hired a stenographer to type one of his plays for Professor Baker's class. When her bill was far more than he could pay, he simply did nothing until the woman brought suit against him. His attorney was his Boston uncle, Henry A. Westall, and Westall probably was responsible for the proceedings. He let the typist win a judgment against Wolfe; then, in a flourish worthy of Bascom Hawke, Westall informed the court that Wolfe was still a minor. Since Westall, as Wolfe's "guardian pro tem," had not authorized the typing, the claim was invalid. Finally Professor Baker was asked to referee the case, and a settlement was made (*Letters*, p. 48). Wolfe did not give in easily, even when he was at fault.

Wolfe was a man who appeared to be larger than life, a fact appropriate to his great ambition. His death at age thirty-seven has given him the aura of youth; unlike his brothers and sisters, he was driven to art, and, as he wrote in *The Story of a Novel*, he "wanted fame, as every youth who ever wrote must want it, and yet fame was a shining, bright, and most uncertain thing." The fame came early. In 1936, two years before Wolfe's death, his mother wrote John Terry that much of her time was taken up in talking to strangers. These people came to Asheville to see the house where Wolfe lived; they wanted to talk to her about him and his work.[9] Almost ten years after Wolfe died, Aline Bernstein still spoke of their extraordinary relationship and referred to the glory that she felt in their love. Such an experience was, she thought, rare. But it was Max Perkins, that distinguished editor, with his characteristic New England reserve, who regarded Wolfe with the highest esteem of all. Perkins felt that at the heart of Wolfe's being was an "unconquerable archangel," a force that somehow set him apart. Judgments about him could not be made simply or in traditional terms.[10]

Wolfe was a man who expended inordinate energy in life and in art; his great compulsion for experience and for capturing that experience in art is undoubtedly responsible for the successes, as well as the failures, of his fiction. In his work he created 1,037 named characters and dozens of unnamed ones; he presents people of twenty foreign nationalities, as well as blacks, Jews, and Indians (Reeves, p. 132). He remains an important spokesman for the 1930s, since he portrayed many of the social, artistic, and political concerns of that decade. Most of all, though, Wolfe is important in conveying the sense of a lost past; in fiction, he successfully rendered the emotions of loneliness, sorrow, alienation, love, and lost love. A rite of passage his works may be for adolescents, but he is far more, as Faulkner saw. He could indeed envision the American novel that would encompass generations and centuries. He will continue to make many readers say of his characters and of their adventures and experiences, "I, too, have been there. I, too, have felt as they have felt."[11]

In his notebook kept from August 30, 1936, until late September 1936, Wolfe wrote the line, "My name is Wolfe; I am an American" (*Notebooks*, II:832). His name, "Wolfe," identifies him with his family and with his native region; "American" speaks of his abiding loyalty and his penchant to celebrate the country in spite of its shortcomings and failures. He was, take him all in all, a spokesman for the South and for America. And if he is judged a failed artist, he was nevertheless a man of great talent who, when subject matter, length, and style were harmonious, produced fiction of the first order.

Notes

1. THE WRITER FROM ASHEVILLE

1. The Old Kentucky Home is now a North Carolina State Memorial and is open to the public.
2. Andrew Turnbull, *Thomas Wolfe* (New York: Scribner's, 1967), p. 7.
3. The children suffered from the family difficulties. Frank displayed tendencies toward juvenile delinquency; Ben was withdrawn and sardonic; Fred and Tom stuttered; Fred, Mabel and Tom were all compulsive talkers. For further discussion, see Richard S. Kennedy, *The Window of Memory: The Literary Career of Thomas Wolfe* (Chapel Hill: University of North Carolina Press, 1962).
4. Louis D. Rubin, Jr., *The Faraway Country: Writers of the Modern South* (Seattle: University of Washington Press, 1963), p. 72.
5. John Hagen, "Time, Death, and Art in *Look Homeward, Angel*," *Thomas Wolfe Review*, 6 (1982):13.
6. CW1. The Thomas Wolfe Collection, John Terry Notes. University of North Carolina Library at Chapel Hill.
7. See Richard Walser, *Thomas Wolfe Undergraduate* (Durham, N.C.: Duke University Press, 1977), for a full account of Wolfe's Chapel Hill years.

8. Frederick Koch directed the Carolina Playmakers, who staged Wolfe's play, *The Return of Buck Gavin*. Later, much to Wolfe's chagrin, Koch included this play in his *Carolina Folk Plays*. Koch's influence on Wolfe was not entirely helpful. As Turnbull notes, Koch was a teacher long on encouragement and short on discipline; he told his students, "We don't need any rules— we write from our hearts" (p. 32). Ignoring rules was not advice Wolfe needed.

9. *The Letters of Thomas Wolfe to His Mother*, ed. C. Hugh Holman and Sue Fields Ross (New York: Scribner's, 1968), p. 64.

10. John Halberstadt's recent article, "The Making of Thomas Wolfe's Posthumous Novels" (*Yale Review*, 70 [1980]:79–94), as well as his subsequent letters and notes, has not brought news to Wolfe scholars. The problem of the editing of these works has long been discussed, particularly by Louis D. Rubin, Jr., in *The Faraway Country* and Richard S. Kennedy in *The Window of Memory*. Kennedy has more recently addressed the issue in "The 'Wolfegate' Affair," *Harvard Magazine*, 84 (September–October 1981):48–54.

11. See Elizabeth Nowell, *Thomas Wolfe: A Biography* (Garden City, N.Y.: Doubleday, 1960), pp. 82 ff., for a full discussion.

12. *The Letters of Thomas Wolfe*, ed. Elizabeth Nowell (New York: Scribner's, 1956), p. 109.

13. For a thorough discussion of Aline Berstein's theatrical career, see Carole Klein, *Aline* (New York: Harper & Row, 1979).

14. Madeleine Boyd, "The Discovery of a Genius," Introd. by Elizabeth Evans (Sandusky, Ohio: Eric Bay Company, 1981), A Thomas Wolfe Society Publication. See the introduction for a discussion of Boyd's association with Wolfe.

15. A. Scott Berg, *Max Perkins: Editor of Genius* (New York: Dutton, 1978).

16. *Editor to Author: The Letters of Maxwell E. Perkins*, ed. John Hall Wheelock (New York: Scribner's, 1950), p. 247.

17. C. Hugh Holman, *The Loneliness at the Core: Studies in Thomas Wolfe* (Baton Rouge: Louisiana State University Press, 1975), p. 50.

18. *The Story of a Novel*, originally a lecture, was cut by Elizabeth Nowell and published in the *Saturday Review of Literature* in three installments, December 14, 21, and 28, 1935. Later Wolfe restored the cuts and added an important new section. An edition of 3,000 copies of this version was published on April 21, 1936. Bernard De Voto's article, "Genius Is Not Enough," appeared almost immediately in the *Saturday Review of Literature*, April 25, 1936.

19. On April 23, 1935, Wolfe, jubilant over the news that Elizabeth Nowell had sold four of his stories, wrote her from Europe: "The news, if true, is swell, but I don't know where the hell you *found* the four stories (*Letters*, p. 449).

20. *The Notebooks of Thomas Wolfe*, ed. Richard S. Kennedy and Paschal Reeves (Chapel Hill: University of North Carolina Press, 1970), II: 449.

21. On June 9, 1923, while still a student at Harvard, Wolfe wrote his mother a postcard from New York: "I came in this morning and have spent the day at the Metropolitan Art Museum. It is glorious, wonderful, beautiful" (*Letters to His Mother*, p. 47). Interestingly, a check of the notebook as well as of the letters edited by Nowell and those edited by Holman and Ross, reveal only one mention of any of America's "old masters." In a notebook passage, Wolfe does call John Singleton Copley "one of the greatest portrait painters that ever lived" (II:501).

22. C. Hugh Holman, "Thomas Wolfe's Berlin," *Saturday Review*, 100 (March 11, 1967):67.

23. A longer version of "I Have a Thing to Tell You" appears in *You Can't Go Home Again*. See Kennedy, *The Window of Memory*, pp. 325–333, for a discussion of Wolfe's political awakening, which this short novel reflects.

24. bMS Am1883. The Thomas Wolfe Collection of William B. Wisdom, Harvard College Library. At the top of the cartoon is this handwritten note: "Harold, please pass this on to Tom. He might miss it and it is amusing. I am still laid up— getting sort of disgusted with living—rather with *not* living. Best wishes always. Cade." At the side is this handwritten message: "Tom. What strange power is this you have over the women?"

25. Faulkner wrote a letter to Professor Richard Walser in which he said, "Among his and my contemporaries, I rated Wolfe first because we had all failed but Wolfe had made the best failure because he had tried hardest to say the most." Quoted in *The Enigma of Thomas Wolfe: Biographical and Critical Selections*, ed. Richard Walser (Cambridge: Harvard University Press, 1953), p. vii.

26. *Letters of Flannery O'Connor: The Habit of Being* (New York: Farrar, Straus & Giroux, 1979), p. 385.

2. *LOOK HOMEWARD, ANGEL* and *OF TIME AND THE RIVER*: "THE APPLE TREE, THE SINGING, AND THE GOLD"

1. Richard S. Kennedy, *The Window of Memory. The Literary Career of Thomas Wolfe* (Chapel

Hill: University of North Carolina Press, 1962),
pp. 97–107.

2. *The Letters of Thomas Wolfe*, ed. Elizabeth
Nowell (New York: Scribner's, 1956), pp. 71–72.

3. "London Tower" was reprinted in 1980 by the
Thomas Wolfe Society.

4. C. Hugh Holman, *The Loneliness at the Core:
Studies in Thomas Wolfe* (Baton Rouge: Louisiana State University Press, 1975), p. 30.

5. *The Notebooks of Thomas Wolfe*, ed. Richard S.
Kennedy and Paschal Reeves (Chapel Hill: University of North Carolina Press, 1970), II: 940–
941.

6. The earliest study of Wolfe's theory of time is
the still valuable article by Margaret Church,
"Thomas Wolfe: Dark Time," *PMLA*, 64
(1949):629–638.

7. For further discussion of this and other song tags
in *Look Homeward, Angel*, see Elizabeth Evans,
"Music in *Look Homeward, Angel*," *Southern
Literary Journal*, 8 (1976):62–74.

8. John Hagen, "Structure, Theme, and Metaphor
in Thomas Wolfe's *Look Homeward, Angel*,"
American Literature, 53 (1981):269–270.

9. John Earl Bassett has recently noted that "Southern reviewers were quicker to express reservations toward *Look Homeward, Angel* in 1929,
but on the whole were no more negative than
reviewers in the North. Of seventeen known reviews in the North, four were predominantly
negative; of fifteen in the South, no more than
three were. In any case, Wolfe had become a recognized new talent, one who would soon be
praised by Sinclair Lewis, Hugh Walpole, Richard Aldington, and William Faulkner." ("The
Critical Reception of *Look Homeward, Angel*,"
Thomas Wolfe Review, 6 [1982]:45–49).

10. *The New York Times Book Review* of December

2, 1979, published James Atlas's "The Case for Thomas Wolfe." Acknowledging the flurry the novel caused at its publication, Atlas notes the later reaction: "Since then, Wolfe's reputation has worn thin, and he is now generally considered an archaic figure whom only adolescents can appreciate—a literary *rite de passage* as immutable as puberty" (p. 3).

11. Scribner's published Johnson's study under the title *Hungry Gulliver: An English Appraisal of Thomas Wolfe* (1948).

12. bMS Am1833. Manuscript Letter of Pamela Hansford Johnson to Thomas Wolfe. The Thomas Wolfe Collection of William B. Wisdom, Harvard College Library.

13. Robert Penn Warren, "A Note on the Hamlet of Thomas Wolfe," in *Thomas Wolfe: Three Decades of Criticism*, ed. Leslie A. Field (New York: New York University Press, 1968), p. 216.

14. William Styron, "The Shade of Thomas Wolfe," in *Thomas Wolfe: A Collection of Critical Essays*, ed. Louis D. Rubin, Jr. (Englewood Cliffs, N.J.: Prentice-Hall, 1973), p. 105. Styron himself made considerable use of Wolfe and his career in his own recent novel, *Sophie's Choice*.

15. bMS Am1833.1. Manuscript Letter of Elizabeth Lemmon to Thomas Wolfe. The Thomas Wolfe Collection of William B. Wisdom. Harvard College Library.

16. The episode of the Coulson family appeared as "The House of the Far and Lost," *Scribner's Magazine*, 96 (August 1934):71–81. It was part of "No Door," a 19,000-word piece *Scribner's Magazine* found too long to publish in a single issue. The opening of this original manuscript appeared in *From Death to Morning* and was also entitled, "No Door." Versions of other parts appeared in five different places in *Of Time and*

the River and in one place in *You Can't Go Home Again* (see Chapter 4). The original text of 19,000 words did not reach print until 1961 when C. Hugh Holman edited and published *The Short Novels of Thomas Wolfe*. This edition is invaluable; readers should consult the head-notes for full publication history.

17. In *The Loneliness at the Core*, Holman points out that the issue in dealing with *Of Time and the River* is not one of genre but of point of view. About the passage on time, "Play us a tune on an unbroken spinet," Holman says, "Lifted out as a prose poem, this section is magnificent. As an episode in a third-person novel it is confusing. As a retrospective account by a first-person narrator it would have authority and dramatic propriety" (p. 83).

18. In his long letter to Max Perkins of December 15, 1936, Wolfe wrote, "Like many another young man who came under the influence of that remarkable work, I wrote my 'Ulysses' book and got it published too. . . . Like Mr. Joyce, I am going to write as I please, and this time, no one is going to cut me unless I want them to" (*Letters*, pp. 586–587).

19. Virginia Woolf, "The Novel of Consciousness," in *The Modern Tradition: Backgrounds in Modern Literature*, ed. Richard Ellmann and Charles Feidelson, Jr. (New York: Oxford University Press, 1963), p. 122.

3. *THE WEB AND THE ROCK* and *YOU CAN'T GO HOME AGAIN*: NOVELS OF MAGNIFICENT FRAGMENTS

1. Bruce R. McElderry, *Thomas Wolfe* (New Haven: Twayne Publishers, 1964), p. 103.

2. See Richard S. Kennedy, *The Window of Memory: The Literary Career of Thomas Wolfe* (Chapel Hill: University of North Carolina Press, 1962), pp. 299–311, for a full discussion.

3. The story was published in *The Saturday Evening Post* on September 11, 1937.

4. Herbert Muller, *Thomas Wolfe* (Norfolk, Conn.: New Directions, 1947), p. 121.

5. Paschal Reeves, "Esther Jack as Muse," in *Thomas Wolfe: Three Decades of Criticism*, ed. Leslie A. Field (New York: New York University Press, 1968), p. 221.

6. C. Hugh Holman, *The Loneliness at the Core: Studies in Thomas Wolfe* (Baton Rouge: Louisiana State University Press, 1975), p. 17.

7. Clyde C. Clements, Jr., "Symbolic Patterns in *You Can't Go Home Again*," in *Thomas Wolfe: Three Decades of Criticism*, ed. Leslie A. Field (New York: New York University Press, 1968), p. 229.

8. "The Party at Jack's" was published in *Scribner's Magazine*, 105 (May 1939):14–16; 40–42; 58–62. "I Have a Thing to Tell You" was published in *The New Republic*, 90 (March 10, 17, and 24, 1937):132–136; 159–164; 202–207.

9. Clyde Clements's term, "symbolic patterns," suggests this same idea.

10. Wolfe borrowed a Jack Keefe malapropism from Ring Lardner's *You Know Me Al*, a book he read and liked.

11. This episode depicting a discrepancy between the reporter's questions and his published article (*You Can't Go Home Again*) is similar to the misrepresentation of Eugene that the Countess persists in making (*Of Time and the River*).

12. Wolfe may here be paying Perkins a compliment. In his biography, *Max Perkins: Editor of Genius*, A. Scott Berg notes that *War and Peace*

was Perkins's favorite book, one he considered "the paragon of literature" and often sent to his authors.

13. Wolfe uses the real suicide of as man identified only as C. Green to depict the prevalence of death during this era. Green jumped from the Admiral Drake Hotel in New York; and Wolfe devotes Chapter 29 in *You Can't Go Home Again* to the mystery surrounding the man and his death.

4. *FROM DEATH TO MORNING, THE HILLS BEYOND*, AND THE SHORT NOVELS: FAILURE, SUCCESS?

1. Richard Walser, *Thomas Wolfe Undergraduate* (Durham, N.C.: Duke University Press, 1977).
2. *The Letters of Thomas Wolfe*, ed. Elizabeth Nowell (New York: Scribner's, 1956), p. 11.
3. CW. The Thomas Wolfe Collections. University of North Carolina Library at Chapel Hill.
4. Jerry Rice, "Thomas Wolfe's *Mannerhouse*," *Thomas Wolfe Review*, 6 (1982):25–26.
5. CW1. The Thomas Wolfe Collection. John Terry Notes. University of North Carolina Library at Chapel Hill.
6. Edward A. Bloom, "Critical Commentary on 'Only the Dead Know Brooklyn,'" in *Thomas Wolfe: Three Decades of Criticism*, ed. Leslie A. Field (New York: New York University Press, 1968), pp. 269–272. Bloom suggests that Wolfe is creating allegory to show "Brooklyn as modern confused society which suffocates individuality."
7. Sharon Doten, "Thomas Wolfe's 'No Door':

Some Textual Questions," *Publications of the Bibliographical Society of America*, 68, No. 1 (January–March 1974):45–52. Doten argues that definitive texts for many of these stories still need to be established.

8. In 1945, Mrs. Wolfe visited John Terry's class at New York University. Among the things she discussed with his students were the mystic voices she claimed to have heard. These voices said, "Two . . . two; twenty . . . twenty" and Julia Wolfe took them to be the two robbers as well as the twins and their birth date. See "*Look Homeward, Angel*," *Saturday Review of Literature*, 29 (January 6, 1946):13–14; 31–32 (an interview transcribed by Ruth Davis).

9. See C. Hugh Holman, *The Loneliness at the Core: Studies in Thomas Wolfe* (Baton Rouge: Louisiana State University Press, 1975), pp. 60–61.

10. The publisher's note in *Of Time and the River* announced that it was the second in a series of six novels. The other five titles were listed, along with the time periods they covered. Fourth in that list was *The Hills Beyond Pentland* (1838–1926). In this note, Aswell points out that except for a few unimportant details, the fragment he included bears no resemblance "to anything Tom ever wrote or intended for *The Hills Beyond Pentland*" (p. 385). The similarity in the titles is doubtless one of the "unimportant details."

11. When Wolfe finally returned to Asheville in 1937, he visited John Westall, a half brother of his grandfather. The old man's recollections about the Civil War gave Wolfe the subject matter for "Chickamauga."

12. In "*The Hills Beyond*: A Folk Novel of America" (in *Thomas Wolfe: Three Decades of Criticism*,

ed. Leslie A. Field [New York: New York University Press, 1968], pp. 241–252], Leslie Field documents the sources of folklore elements in the novel fragment. Field points out that Bear Joyner represents frontier and Yankee folklore characters. Furthermore, Joyner has a third dimension—book learning. His learning to read at age forty, Field notes, separates Bear from others around him.

13. Cf. Louis D. Rubin, Jr., *Thomas Wolfe: The Weather of His Youth* (Baton Rouge: Louisiana State University Press, 1955), p. 165.

14. *The Short Novels of Thomas Wolfe*, ed. C. Hugh Holman (New York: Scribner's, 1961).

15. See C. Hugh Holman, "Thomas Wolfe's Berlin," *Saturday Review*, 60 (March 11, 1967):66, 69, 80.

16. Max Perkins, "Thomas Wolfe," *Scribner's Magazine*, 105 (May 1939):5.

17. *Scribner's Magazine*, 105 (May 1939), 17.

5. "MY NAME IS WOLFE: I AM AN AMERICAN"

1. *The Letters of Thomas Wolfe*, ed. Elizabeth Nowell (New York: Scribner's, 1956), p. 109.

2. See *A Stone, A Leaf, A Door: Poems by Thomas Wolfe*, selected and arranged in verse by John S. Barnes (New York: Scribner's 1955).

3. Richard S. Kennedy, *The Window of Memory: The Literary Career of Thomas Wolfe* (Chapel Hill: University of North Carolina Press, 1962), p. 340.

4. See also Bruce R. McElderry, Jr., "The Durable Humor of *Look Homeward, Angel*," in *Thomas Wolfe: Three Decades of Criticism*, ed. Leslie A. Field (New York: New York University Press, 1968), pp. 189–194.

5. Paschal Reeves, *Thomas Wolfe's Albatross: Race and Nationality in America* (Athens: University of Georgia Press, 1968), pp. 135–136.

6. See also *The Notebooks of Thomas Wolfe*, ed. Richard S. Kennedy and Paschal Reeves (Chapel Hill: University of North Carolina Press, 1970), II: 620.

7. Edward C. Aswell, "A Note on Thomas Wolfe," in *The Hills Beyond* (New York: Harper, 1941), pp. 349–386.

8. Floyd Watkins, *Thomas Wolfe's Characters* (Norman: University of Oklahoma Press, 1957), p. 45.

9. CW1. The Thomas Wolfe Collection. John Terry Notes. University of North Carolina Library at Chapel Hill.

10. *Ibid.*

11. C. Hugh Holman, "20th Century American Novel: *Look Homeward, Angel*" (De Land, Florida: Everett/Edwards Cassette Curriculum, 1971).

Bibliography

WORKS BY THOMAS WOLFE

Novels

Look Homeward, Angel. New York: Scribner's, 1929.

Of Time and the River. New York: Scribner's, 1935.

The Web and the Rock. New York: Harper, 1939.

You Can't Go Home Again. New York: Harper, 1940.

Shorter Works

From Death to Morning. New York: Scribner's, 1935.

The Story of a Novel. New York: Scribner's, 1936.

A Note on Experts: Dexter Vespasian Joyner. New York: House of Books, 1939.

The Hills Beyond. New York: Harper, 1941.

Thomas Wolfe's Purdue Speech: "Writing and Living." Ed. William Braswell and Leslie A. Field. Purdue University Studies, 1964.

The Crisis in Industry (essay). 1919. Rpt. Winston-Salem: Palaemon Press, 1978.

A Prologue to America, ed. Aldo P. Magi, 1938. Rpt. Athens, Ohio: Croissant, 1978.

Drama

The Return of Buck Gavin: The Tragedy of a Mountain Outlaw. In Frederick H. Koch, ed., *Carolina Folk-Plays*, Second Series. New York: Holt, 1924.

The Third Night. In Frederick H. Koch, ed., *Carolina Folk-Plays*. New York: Holt, 1941.

Mannerhouse. New York: Harper, 1948.

The Mountains: A Play in One Act and *The Mountains: A Drama in Three Acts and a Prologue.* Ed. with an Introd. by Pat M. Ryan. Chapel Hill: University of North Carolina Press, 1970.

The Streets of Durham. Ed. with an Introd. by Richard Walser. Raleigh, N.C.: Wolf's Head Press, 1982.

Welcome to Our City: A Play in Ten Scenes. Ed. with an Introd. by Richard S. Kennedy. Baton Rouge: Louisiana State University Press, 1983.

Notebooks, Journals, Letters

A Western Journal. Pittsburgh: University of Pittsburgh Press, 1951.

The Correspondence of Thomas Wolfe and Homer Andrew Watt. Ed. Oscar Cargill and Thomas Clark Pollack. New York: 1954.

The Letters of Thomas Wolfe. Ed. Elizabeth Nowell. New York: Scribner's, 1956.

The Letters of Thomas Wolfe to His Mother. Ed. C. Hugh Holman and Sue Fields Ross. Chapel Hill: University of North Carolina Press, 1968. (Supersedes the 1943 edition edited by John Terry)

The Notebooks of Thomas Wolfe. Ed. Richard S. Kennedy and Paschal Reeves. Chapel Hill: University of North Carolina Press, 1970.

Beyond Love and Loyalty: The Letters of Thomas Wolfe and Elizabeth Nowell. Ed. Richard S. Kennedy. Chapel Hill: University of North Carolina Press, 1983.

The Letters of Thomas Wolfe and Aline Bernstein. Ed. Suzanne Stutman. Chapel Hill: University of North Carolina Press, 1983.

Selections from Wolfe's Works

The Face of a Nation: Poetical Passages from the Writings of Thomas Wolfe. Sel. and ed. with an Introd. by John Hall Wheelock. New York: Scribner's, 1939.

A Stone, A Leaf, A Door: Poems by Thomas Wolfe. Sel. and arr. in verse by John S. Barnes, with a Foreword by Louis Untermeyer. New York: Scribner's, 1945.

The Portable Thomas Wolfe. Ed. Maxwell Geismar. New York: Viking, 1946.

The Thomas Wolfe Reader. Ed. with an Introd. and notes by C. Hugh Holman. New York: Scribner's, 1962.

Thomas Wolfe: The Autobiography of an American Novelist. Ed. Leslie Field. Cambridge: Harvard University Press, 1983.

BIBLIOGRAPHIES AND CHECKLISTS

Kauffman, Bernice. "Bibliography of Periodical Articles on Thomas Wolfe." *Bulletin of Bibliography*, 17 (May and August 1942):162–165, 172–190.

Preston, George R., Jr. *Thomas Wolfe: A Bibliography.* New York: Boesen, 1943.

Johnson, Elmer D. *Of Time and Thomas Wolfe: A Bibliography with a Character Index of His Works.* New York: Scarecrow Press, 1959.

Holman, C. Hugh. "Thomas Wolfe: A Bibliographical Study." *Texas Studies in Literature and Language*, 1 (Autumn 1959):427–445.

Beebe, Maurice, and Leslie A. Field. "Criticism of Thomas Wolfe: A Selected Checklist." *Modern Fiction Studies*, 11 (Autumn 1965):315–328. (Thomas Wolfe Special Number, rpt. in Field, *Thomas Wolfe: Three Decades of Criticism*, pp. 273–293.

Kennedy, Richard S. "Thomas Wolfe." In Louis D. Rubin, Jr., ed., *A Bibliographical Guide to the Study of Southern Literature*. Baton Rouge: Louisiana State University Press, 1969, pp. 329–332.

Reeves, Paschal. *Checklist of Thomas Wolfe*. Columbus, Ohio: Charles E. Merrill, 1969.

Johnson, Elmer D. *Thomas Wolfe. A Checklist*. Kent, Ohio: Kent State University Press, 1970.

Phillipson, John S. *Thomas Wolfe: A Reference Guide*. Boston: G. K. Hall, 1977.

Teicher, Morton I. "A Bibliography of Books with Selections by Thomas Wolfe." *Bulletin of Bibliography*, 38 (October–December 1981):194–208.

Johnston, Carol. *Thomas Wolfe. A Descriptive Bibliography*. Pittsburgh: University of Pittsburgh Press Series in Bibliography (forthcoming).

PUBLICATIONS OF THE THOMAS WOLFE SOCIETY

Wolfe, Thomas. *The Proem to "O Lost."* Ed. John L. Idol, Jr., 1980.

———. *London Tower*. Ed. Aldo P. Magi. 1980.

Boyd, Madeleine. *Thomas Wolfe: The Discovery of a Genius*. Ed. Aldo P. Magi, with an Introd. by Elizabeth Evans. 1981.

Wolfe, Thomas. *The Streets of Durham*. With an Introd. by Richard Walser. Raleigh, N.C.: Wolf's Head Press, 1982.

Wolfe, Thomas. *K-19. Salvaged Pieces*. Ed. John L. Idol. Columbia, S.C.: R. L. Bryan Company, 1983.

WORKS ABOUT THOMAS WOLFE

NOTE: Readers should consult the bibliographies in *PMLA, American Literature,* and the *Thomas Wolfe Review* for current bibliographical information.

Professor David Herbert Donald is at work on a biography of Thomas Wolfe.

Biographies and Memoirs about Wolfe; Works Related to Wolfe

Adams, Agatha Boyd. *Thomas Wolfe: Carolina Student*. Chapel Hill: University of North Carolina Library, 1950.

Armstrong, Anne W. "As I Saw Thomas Wolfe." *Arizona Quarterly*, 2 (1946):5–14.

Austin, Neal F. *A Biography of Thomas Wolfe*. Austin, Texas: Roger Beacham, 1968.

Berg, A. Scott. *Max Perkins: Editor of Genius*. New York: Dutton, 1978.

Cane, Melville. "Thomas Wolfe: A Memoir." *American Scholar*, 41 (1972):637–642.

Daniels, Jonathan. *Thomas Wolfe: October Recollections*. Columbia, S.C.: Bostwick and Thornley, 1961.

Klein, Carole. *Aline*. New York: Harper & Row, 1979.

Magi, Aldo P., and Richard Walser, eds. *Thomas Wolfe Our Friend: The Journal of Clayton and Kathleen Hoagland*. Athens, Ohio: Croissant, 1979.

Norwood, Hayden. *The Marble Man's Wife: Thomas Wolfe's Mother*. New York: Scribner's, 1947.

Nowell, Elizabeth. *Thomas Wolfe: A Biography*. Garden City, N.Y.: Doubleday, 1960.

Pollock, Thomas Clark, and Oscar Cargill. *Thomas Wolfe at Washington Square*. New York: New York University Press, 1954.

Raynolds, Robert. *Thomas Wolfe: Memoir of a Friendship*. Austin: University of Texas Press, 1965.

Turnbull, Andrew. *Thomas Wolfe*. New York: Scribner's, 1967.

Wheaton, Mabel Wolfe, and LeGette Blythe. *Thomas Wolfe and His Family*. Garden City, N.Y.: Doubleday, 1961.

Wheelock, John Hall, ed. *Editor to Author: The Letters of Maxwell E. Perkins*. New York: Scribner's, 1950.

Books, Pamphlets, Special Issues of Journals

Beebe, Maurice, ed. *Thomas Wolfe Special Number, Modern Fiction Studies*, 11:3 (Autumn 1965).

Champion, Myra, comp. *The Lost World of Thomas Wolfe*. Asheville: The Thomas Wolfe Memorial. Rev. ed., 1975.

Gurko, Leo. *Thomas Wolfe: Beyond the Romantic Ego*. New York: Crowell, 1974.

Holman, C. Hugh. *Thomas Wolfe*. Minneapolis: University of Minnesota Press, 1960.

———. *The Loneliness at the Core: Studies in Thomas Wolfe*. Baton Rouge: Louisiana State University Press, 1975.

Johnson, Pamela Hansford. *Hungry Gulliver: An English Critical Appraisal of Thomas Wolfe*. New York: Scribner's, 1948.

Kennedy, Richard S. *The Window of Memory: The Literary Career of Thomas Wolfe*. Chapel Hill: University of North Carolina Press, 1962.

McElderry, Bruce R. *Thomas Wolfe*. New Haven: College and University Press, 1964.

Marx, Samuel. *Thomas Wolfe and Hollywood*. Athens, Ohio: Croissant, 1980.

Muller, Herbert J. *Thomas Wolfe*. Norfolk, Conn.: New Directions, 1947.

Payne, Ladell. *Thomas Wolfe*. Austin, Texas: Steck-Vaughn, 1969.

Reeves, Paschal. *Thomas Wolfe's Albatross: Race and Nationality in America*. Athens: University of Georgia Press, 1968.

Rubin, Louis D., Jr. *Thomas Wolfe: The Weather of His Youth*. Baton Rouge: Louisiana State University Press, 1955.

Ryssel, Fritz Heinrich. *Thomas Wolfe*. Trans. Helen Sebba. New York: Ungar, 1972.

Snyder, William U. *Thomas Wolfe: Ulysses and Narcissus*. Athens: Ohio University Press, 1971.

Steele, Richard. *Thomas Wolfe: A Psychoanalytic Literary Criticism*. Philadelphia: Dorrance, 1976.

Walser, Richard. *Thomas Wolfe. An Introduction and Interpretation*. New York: Barnes & Noble, 1961.

———. *Thomas Wolfe Undergraduate*. Durham, N.C.: Duke University Press, 1977.

———. *Thomas Wolfe's Pennsylvania*. Athens, Ohio: Croissant, 1978.

———. *The Wolfe Family in Raleigh*. Raleigh, N.C.: Wolf's Head Press, 1976.

Watkins, Floyd C. *Thomas Wolfe's Characters*. Norman: University of Oklahoma Press, 1957.

Collections of Critical Essays

Field, Leslie A., ed. *Thomas Wolfe: Three Decades of Criticism*. New York: New York University Press, 1968.

Holman, C. Hugh. *The World of Thomas Wolfe*. A Scribner's Research Anthology. New York: Scribner's, 1962.

Jones, H. G., ed. *Thomas Wolfe of North Carolina*. Chapel Hill: North Caroliniana Society, 1982.

Reeves, Paschal, comp. *Studies in Look Homeward, Angel*. Columbus, Ohio: Charles E. Merrill, 1970.

————, ed. *Thomas Wolfe and the Glass of Time*. Athens: University of Georgia Press, 1971.

Rubin, Louis D., Jr., ed. *Thomas Wolfe: A Collection of Critical Essays*. Englewood Cliffs, N.J.: Prentice-Hall, 1973.

Walser, Richard, ed. *The Enigma of Thomas Wolfe: Biographical and Critical Selections*. Cambridge: Harvard University Press, 1953.

Selected Articles

Albrecht, W. P. "Time as Unity in the Novels of Thomas Wolfe." *New Mexico Quarterly Review*, 19 (Autumn 1949):320–329.

Bassett, John Earl. "The Critical Reception of *Look Homeward, Angel*." *Thomas Wolfe Review*, 6 (1982):45–49.

Bredahl, A. Carl, Jr. "*Look Homeward, Angel*: Individuation and Articulation." *Southern Literary Journal*, 6 (1973):47–58.

Church, Margaret. "Thomas Wolfe: Dark Time." In *Time and Reality: Studies in Contemporary Fiction*. Chapel Hill: University of North Carolina Press, 1963. (A modification of "Thomas Wolfe: Dark Time," *PMLA*, 64 (1949):629–638.)

Cowley, Malcolm. "Wolfe: Homo Scribens." In *A Second Flowering: Works and Days of the Lost Generation*. New York: Viking, 1973.

Evans, Elizabeth. "Music in *Look Homeward, Angel*." *Southern Literary Journal*, 8 (1976):62–74.

Field, Leslie A. "Thomas Wolfe and the Kicking Season Again." *South Atlantic Quarterly*, 69 (1970):364–372.

Foster, Ruel E. "Thomas Wolfe's Mountain Gloom and Glory." *American Literature*, 44 (1973):638–647.

Green, Charmian. "Wolfe's Stonecutter Once Again: An Unpublished Episode." *Mississippi Quarterly*, 30 (1977):611–623.

Hagen, John. "Structure, Theme, and Metaphor in Thomas Wolfe's *Look Homeward, Angel*." *American Literature*, 53 (1981):266–285.

———. "Time, Death and Art in *Look Homeward, Angel*." *Thomas Wolfe Review*, 6 (1982):5–19.

Halberstadt, John. "The Making of Thomas Wolfe's Posthumous Novels." *Yale Review*, 70 (1980):79–94.

Holman, C. Hugh. "Europe as Catalyst for Thomas Wolfe." In *Essays in American and English Literature Presented to Bruce Robert McElderry, Jr..* Ed. Max F. Schulz. Athens: Ohio University Press, 1967.

———. "Thomas Wolfe and the Stigma of Autobiography." *Virginia Quarterly Review* 40 (1964):614–625.

Idol, John L., Jr. "Angels and Demons: The Satire of *Look Homeward, Angel*." *Studies in Contemporary Satire*, 1–2 (1976):39–46.

———."The Plays of Thomas Wolfe and Their Links with His Novels." *Mississippi Quarterly*, 22 (1969):95–112.

———. "Thomas Wolfe and Jonathan Swift." *South Carolina Review*, 8 (1975):43–54.

———. "Thomas Wolfe and Painting." *Re: Arts and Letters*, 2 (1969):14–20.

Kennedy, Richard S. "Thomas Wolfe's Last Manuscript." *Harvard Library Bulletin*, 23 (April 1975):203–211.

Millichap, Joseph P. "Narrative Structure and Symbolic Imagery in *Look Homeward, Angel.*" *Southern Humanities Review*, 7 (1973):295–303.

Rice, Jerry. "Thomas Wolfe's *Mannerhouse.*" *Thomas Wolfe Review*, 6 (1982):25–34.

Skipp, Francis E. "*Of Time and the River*: The Final Editing." *Publications of the Bibliographical Society of America*, 64 (1970):313–322.

Thompson, Betty. "Thomas Wolfe: Two Decades of Criticism." *South Atlantic Quarterly*, 49 (1950):378–392.

Walser, Richard. "On Faulkner's Putting Wolfe First." *South Atlantic Quarterly*, 78 (1979):172–181.

————. "The McCoy Papers." *Thomas Wolfe Review*, 5 (1981):1–6.

Wank, Martin. "Thomas Wolfe: Two More Decades of Criticism." *South Atlantic Quarterly*, 69 (1970):244–256.

Watkins, Floyd C. "Thomas Wolfe and Asheville Again and Again and Again . . . " *Southern Literary Journal*, 10 (1977):31–55.

Index

"An Angel on the Porch," 132

American Mercury, 128

Asheville *Citizen,* 35, 36

The Aspern Papers (James), 19

Aswell, Edward, 8, 14, 65, 82, 98, 117, 159, 160

Baker, George Pierce, 6–7, 21, 96, 101, 162

Basso, Hamilton, 31

Berg, A. Scott, 15, 16

Bernstein, Aline, 9, 10–14, 20, 22, 26, 79, 89, 153, 163

Boni and Liveright, 79

"Boom Town," 17, 128

Boston Museum of Fine Art, 22

Boyd, Ernest, 14, 79, 159

Boyd, Madeleine, 14, 15, 17, 18, 31, 79, 161

Brueghel, Pieter, 80, 153

"The Bums at Sunset," 101, 103–104

Calder, Alexander, 89

"The Canonization," (Donne), 153

"Chickamauga," 117, 121–122, 128

"The Child by Tiger," 73, 74

"Circus at Dawn," 101

Concerning Honest Bob, 96

Cosmopolitan, 100, 101, 102

Crawford, Annie Laurie, 32

"Dark in the Forest, Strange as Time," 105, 107

"Death the Proud Brother," 108, 111–114, 128

DeVoto, Bernard, 16

Emerson, Ralph Waldo, 53

"The Face of War," 108–111

"The Far and Near," 104

Faulkner, William, 31, 163

Fitzgerald, F. Scott, 15, 23, 26, 159

Ford, Ford Madox, 31

From Death to Morning, 7, 66, 101–117, 129

Frye, Northrop, 48

"Gentlemen of the Press," 122–123

"God's Lonely Man," 25, 123

Gordon, Caroline, 31

Gorsline, Douglas, 132

Grove, E. W., 3

"Gulliver," 104

Hagen, John, 43, 44

Harper (publisher), 8

Harper's Bazaar, 101

Harvard University, 6, 29, 38, 46, 96

Hemingway, Ernest, 15, 159

Herrmann, John, 129

The Hills Beyond, 8, 117–128

The Hills Beyond (fragment), 117, 124–127

Hogarth, William, 20, 153

Holman, C. Hugh, 47, 82, 85, 128, 129

"The House of the Far and Lost," 130

Howells, William Dean, 93

"I Have a Thing To Tell You," 22, 33, 83, 131, 132, 137

James, Henry, 19

Jeliffe, Belinda, 28

Johnson, Pamela Hansford, 45

The Journey Down (Bernstein), 14

Joyce, James, 22, 60, 61, 135

"K-19," 16

Kennedy, Richard S., 13, 17, 19, 22, 25, 36, 46, 47, 73, 82, 102

"A Kinsman of His Blood," 123

Klein, Carole, 5, 13

Koch, Frederick, 6, 96

"The Land of Cockaigne" (Brueghel), 80

Lardner, Ring, 15

Lewis, Sinclair, 84, 157

Lewisohn, Alice, 10, 98, 100

Lieber, Maxim, 18

"The Lion at Morning," 123

"London Tower," 36

Losing Battles (Welty), 139

"The Lost Boy," 4, 33, 117, 118–121, 128

Look Homeward, Angel, 4, 7, 14, 15, 22, 27, 30, 32, 33, 36–46, 58, 67, 75, 78, 79, 95, 100, 122, 128, 129, 133, 139, 140, 146, 148, 149, 151, 153, 157, 161
  early titles, 7, 14
  editing of, 15–16
  subtitle, 37

"Lycidas" (Milton), 37

McCoy, George, 35, 36

McElderry, Bruce R., 65

Mannerhouse, 97, 98–100
Max Perkins: Editor of Genius (Berg), 15
Meade, Julian, 21, 30
Modern Language Association, 31
Modern Monthly, 101, 108
The Mountains, 96
Muller, Herbert, 27, 75, 82

"No Cure for It," 117, 122
"No Door," 105–108, 130
Neighborhood Playhouse, 98, 100
The New Republic, 22, 32
New York University, Washington Square division, 7, 26
New Yorker, 30, 101
Nowell, Elizabeth, 8, 17–19, 24, 31, 101, 129, 137, 160, 162

O'Connor, Flannery, 33
Of Time and the River, 7, 16, 22, 25, 28, 31, 43, 45–63, 66, 78, 95, 99, 102, 123, 129, 130, 137, 138, 146, 149, 153
Old Kentucky Home (boarding house), 1, 5, 28
"On Leprechauns," 123
"One of the Girls in Our Party," 20, 137
"Only the Dead Know Brooklyn," 103, 107

"The Party at Jack's," 83, 131, 132–133
"Passage to England," 161

Perkins, Maxwell, 8, 9, 10, 14, 15, 16, 17, 18, 25, 47, 48, 84, 98, 100, 131, 147, 159, 161, 163
Porter, Katherine Anne, 31
"A Portrait of Bascom Hawke," 33, 129
A Portrait of the Artist as a Young Man (Joyce), 37

Ransom, John Crowe, 31
The Roadmenders (van Gogh), 62
The Return of Buck Gavin, 96
"The Return of the Prodigal," 123
Roberts, Margaret M., 4, 25, 36, 45, 155, 161

St. Louis Exposition (summer boarding house), 4
Saturday Review of Literature, 16, 18
Scribner's (publisher), 7, 8, 10, 45, 128, 131, 161
   Wolfe's break, 16–17
Scribner's Magazine, 18, 84, 101, 102, 128, 129, 130, 131, 132
Southern Review, 31
The Story of a Novel, 8, 18, 66, 162
Styron, William, 47

Terry, John S., 5, 27, 30, 162
Tate, Allen, 31
"Tiger! Tiger!" (Blake), 74

"The Train and the City,"
    128
Tristram Shandy (Sterne),
    37, 61
Turnbull, Andrew, 26, 97
Twain, Mark, 93

Ulysses (Joyce), 60, 61,
    103, 135
University of Colorado
    Writers' Conference,
    16, 66
University of North
    Carolina at Chapel
    Hill, 6, 96

"A Valediction of My
    Name in the
    Window" (Donne), 12
van Gogh, Vincent, 153
Vanderbilt, George W., 3
Vanity Fair, 101
The Vicar of Wakefield
    (Goldsmith), 137
*Virginia Quarterly
    Review*, 101

Walser, Richard, 96
Warren, Robert Penn, 31,
    47
The Waste Land (Eliot),
    150, 159
The Web and the Rock, 8,
    9, 28, 49, 66–82, 85,
    137, 138, 142, 153,
    154, 156

The Web of Earth, 33, 101,
    114–117, 121, 129
Welcome to Our City, 10,
    97, 98
Westall, Henry A. (uncle),
    129, 162
Wheaton, Mabel Wolfe
    (sister), 2, 3, 23, 29,
    32, 45
Whitman, Walt, 32, 144
Wilhelm Meister (Goethe),
    37, 38
Wisdom, William B., 29
Wolfe, Julia Elizabeth
    Westall (mother), 1,
    4–5, 13, 14, 24, 27
Wolfe, Thomas Clayton
    attempts at drama, 6–7,
        96–100
    death, 14, 32
    Germany, 22, 83, 91–92,
        131, 158
    lawsuits, 31, 160–162
    lost generation, 49–50,
        159
    teacher, 7, 26
    time, 39
    South, 9, 23, 98–100
    See also specific works
Wolfe, William Oliver
    (father), 1, 2, 6, 14
Woolf, Virginia, 61

*You Can't Go Home
    Again*, 8, 75, 81, 82–
    94, 123, 130, 138, 147,
    148, 149

Selected list of titles (continued from page ii)

MARIANNE MOORE *Elizabeth Phillips*
VLADIMIR NABOKOV *Donald E. Morton*
THE NOVELS OF HENRY JAMES *Edward Wagenknecht*
JOYCE CAROL OATES *Ellen G. Friedman*
FLANNERY O'CONNOR *Dorothy Tuck McFarland*
JOHN O'HARA *Robert Emmet Long*
GEORGE ORWELL *Roberta Kalechofsky*
KATHERINE ANNE PORTER *John Edward Hardy*
EZRA POUND *Jeannette Lander*
MORDECAI RICHLER *Arnold E. Davidson*
PHILIP ROTH *Judith Jones and Guinevera Nance*
J. D. Salinger *James Lundquist*
ISAAC BASHEVIS SINGER *Irving Malin*
CRISTINA STEAD *Joan Lidoff*
LINCOLN STEFFENS *Robert Stinson*
JOHN STEINBECK *Paul McCarthy*
J. R. R. TOLKIEN *Katharyn F. Crabbe*
LIONEL TRILLING *Edward Joseph Shoben, Jr.*
MARK TWAIN *Robert K. Miller*
JOHN UPDIKE *Suzanne Henning Uphaus*
GORE VIDAL *Robert F. Kiernan*
KURT VONNEGUT *James Lundquist*
ROBERT PENN WARREN *Katherine Snipes*
EUDORA WELTY *Elizabeth Evans*
EDITH WHARTON *Richard H. Lawson*
OSCAR WILDE *Robert Keith Miller*
VIRGINIA WOOLF *Manly Johnson*
RICHARD WRIGHT *David Bakish*

Complete list of titles in the series available from publisher on request.